Tales of Conversion

Adriaan Kamp

For those men and women of faith or good will and that want to help to bring about "Peace and All Good" for Humanity

Basilica di San Francesco and the Sacro Convento in Assisi photographed from the valley in May 2016 by Fr. Silvestro Bejan, OFM Conv., Delegate General for Ecumenism and Interreligious Dialogue and Director of the CEFID (the International Franciscan Center for Dialogue).
http://www.lospiritodiassisi.org/cefid_eng.html

Contents

Specially written for the UN Sustainable Development 2030 Agenda

"Every Country and Every Organization in this world can be improved upon in order to raise the human, social, economic and sustainable development to all".-

Year 2015 has been a Pivot Year in the international order.

First of all, and at the end of 2015, we have seen and witnessed the Climate Change agreement in Paris.

Secondly, and in September of 2015, the UN has agreed and embarked on a ground-breaking program of capacity and capability building in the realms of Sustainable Development.

Thirdly, and not the least, Pope Francis published his encyclical Laudato Si - with his call to humanity to better care for our Common Home, Creation and the dignity and respect for *every* human being.

In all of the above – Stewardship over these transformational programs- in a global, local- government, business and societal setting- is a new (integrated) leadership role to learn.

The booklet "*Tales of Conversion*" is written- for you- and to introduce to you some of the key points of views, insights, conversions and perspectives on this- and that may help or support and encourage you on your way.

It is also to help to raise the conversation(s) we have on said subjects, and to support our shared awareness, insights and sources of inspiration- for our better collective organizations and leadership.

It is by no means exhaustive [1], nor can or does it intend is to be complete.

The booklet is and can only be *our* opening conversation, based on our insights and sources of inspiration, gained thanks to my working practice and experiences[2].

As such – these words desperately needs to become enriched by you and your views on and in this journey.

---

[1] I have on purpose kept this booklet brief and thin. In a follow-up workbook, and directed for the Energy and UN Sustainable Development Professionals, I plan to include more applied strategy, organizational change, science & technology, business model and innovation, energy architecture and sustainability process and methodology details- and which can form part of best practices in the field.
[2] Written on commission

Only by an open and honest dialogue, enquiry and conversations between ourselves- on said subjects – can we expect to see ourselves on the better ways:

Changing Lives.

Making the world a better place.

The "*Tales of Conversion* " is rich in examples and case stories- is written in a light and pragmatic way, and will be accompanied by a rich set of presentation material such that it can be used for educational or professional/ corporate outreach purposes.

A rich set of sources, video material and a literature list will accompany the book.

Finally, and not unimportantly, intent of the organization is to make ourselves available to support the content of this Booklet and make it "come alive" in presentations, conversations and action agenda's around the globe.

Conversion/kən ˈvə ːʃ(ə)n/

the process of changing or causing something to change from one form to another.
the fact of changing one's religion or beliefs or the action of persuading someone else to change theirs.
a successful kick at goal after a try, scoring two points.

The Spirit of Assisi (definition)

1. Peace and All Good

2. Unity in Diversity

3. Listening, dialogue, mediation and understanding:

4. **building common ground - convergence**

Mission Energy for One World (not-for-profit)[3]

Mission Energy for One World focus[4] is supporting and helping customers to learn to integrate the UN sustainable development agenda and Paris Climate Change Agreement into mainstream energy architecture, economic and international trade relations developments.

We have come to see and understand that every Nation and every company has his own history, culture and natural needs for progression.

Stewardship in these programs is hence a new balancing act between Human Development, Economy, Society, Technology, Sustainability and our International relationships.

Helping customers to do this – our mission seeks to combine and unlock some of the better interfaith religion, academic, business and wisdom leadership, including industry capabilities around, and make this available in outreach, interventions, education, consultancy, business-matchmaking, project (opportunity) development.

We recognize as no other that "Our Tone of Voice" matters if we want to progress and advance human, national and/or corporate interests, whilst also taking care of the whole.

Our mission focus is directed towards the realization of *systematic* improvements in the local and global (sustainable, economic and social developments/) system and outlook. As such – we support leadership to define and realize the opportunity space for business and government to succeed in the more whole, holistic and better balanced and interconnected world of today and tomorrow.

A key perspective in our mission approach is that *all* nations and *all* people have a fundamental right for a dignified life and meaning, and that Nature and our relation with Creation forms an integral part in this equation.

We especially care for the poor and deprived, and we believe that in order to help the millions and millions of poor people, we also have to change the Rich and the Elites.

In order to achieve this, and for a growing world population, we may want to improve on our local, regional and global system realizations.

Our working mission helps Leaders to develop a (local and relevant) strategy-balancing Economy, Society and Sustainability needs, and based on this strategy, on how to define and organize (business or national) change and/or opportunities- also based on existing best practices already proven in the

---

[3] Mission will collaborate with Assisi Mission
[4] In collaboration with e.g. Business Universities, Assisi Mission: The Spirit of Assisi

practice of sustainable development, international support organizations and finance.

Energy for One World has been given the opportunity to write this small booklet for you.

Special thanks to Assisi Mission, that has inspired this work to be created, and has supported the creation of this project.

Thank also to all other contributors and my international support group who has made this journey possible

The Spirit of Assisi

I am writing these words from my borrowed laptop computer in a small apartment overlooking the Umbria Valley and in the medieval township of Assisi, in Italy.

I am here to design, author and/or co-create some bridges between the Spirit of Assisi and the words of Pope Francis Encyclical Laudato Si! with that of our modern world and days of Energy and the Un Sustainable Development Agenda.

But I am here also on a small or more longer (work-life) vacation, after my five years in Oslo and Netherlands- building the Energy For One World [5]not-for-profit outreach and consulting practice.

And as I was landing in Assisi for the summer period – now some three weeks ago- a small conversion of me also took place and hold.

It is true that every pebble, every corner, every Church, monastery and Holy shrine of this small and more wonderful little townships at the mountain hill of Subasio- tells a story and breathes a heart-felt warmth, peace, tranquillity and calm.

The streets, people and tourist visitors to Assisi are a welcome sign of the world we aspire to know:

"Peace and All Good".

Those were the words and dreams of the man who has once shaken this little township, now some 800 years ago.

It was Saint Francis, and in his early youth years, decided that "enough was enough": he could no longer see value in the attainment of only material wealth, especially not at the cost of others.

Conversion of Francis eyes and mind came about when he started to observe how poor "the poor and deprived" were actually treated by his father and the wealthy elite of his times-

Conversion of Francis came about as he came to see how seldom "rich and good" the elite and his family has made themselves - in their own days and ways- and how their eyes and ears were turned away and not attuned to the needs of the poor or the earthly beauties that was actually around: the hills and valleys of nature, the beauties and serenities of every plant, animal and species around. Brother Sun and Sister Moon. Our Common Home and Creation.

Conversion of Saint Francis, and as the story (legend?) goes, was also by an act of Grace and God : helping (pure-hearted) Francis to have faith and good will and

---

[5] www.energyforoneworld.com

to *see, hear and find* the courage for conversion – becoming inspired to let go[6] and to become part of a new and better world.

That act is the reason that some 5 million visitors from *all* over the world, and of *all* faith, come to Assisi every year.

That act of faith has become instrumental in the creation of the spirit of Assisi[7], some 800 years later and very much working today.

And the life, conversion and works of Saint Francis (and Santa Clara) has inspired the existence of a 800 year young St Francis' Friars Minor Order, and has given name and birth to our present Holy See of the Catholic Church of Rome.

It has given word and name to the encyclical of Pope Francis on our Common Home and Creation: Laudato Si![8]

So what are the mysteries and message(s) of Saint Francis and Pope Francis bringing us today?

What are we to read in Laudato Si! for our modern days and ways, and what invitation is out there - to us- for our conversion and convergence, or our courage to become part of better leadership over UN Sustainable development?

And what does this Spirit of Assisi means in our day to day in business and governance?

This and some other considerations are part of the journey I plan to take you on, in this small booklet with conversations on conversions and convergence, Laudato Si, the spirit of Assisi and the bridge to the UN Sustainable Development Goals.

It proofs to become an interesting excursion: a deep dive on the path of some meaning, essences and decision making in our present days, life and times.

I welcome you on my (this) path and invite our journey to begin.

Adriaan Kamp- Founder of Energy For One World, September 2016

---

[6] Of all material wealth: vow of poverty

[7] Inter-religious peace building dialogue, initiated by father Maximillian Mizzi, OFM Conv. in 1960 and Pope John Paul II in 1986 in Assisi. The spirit of Assisi stands now for :

1. Peace and All Good
2. Unity in Diversity
3. Listening, dialogue, mediation and understanding: **building common ground (convergence)**

[8] Laudato Si! Is the name of the hymn St Francis wrote on Creation. The title of this hymn has been used by Pope Francis for his famous encyclical on our Common Home (2015)

Our Journey

Let's imagine ourselves in year 2100.

What are we expect to see?

If the UN Sustainable Development Goals and Agenda have been up kept- then at least we are to expect to see a world where a rich diversity of cultures, religions and nations living happily together, sharing One Planet- and see themselves in harmony between themselves and with nature: having achieved truly sustainable and meaningful lives:

Everybody is included, and everybody is of value.

A new balance has been found between the rapidization of our technologies and innovations, societies and economies, and the calm and tranquillity of the natural environment.

Dignity and respect are and have become common good: for each other, and for the relation we have to the rest of Creation.

Somewhere along this journey – we may have achieved to transform the – at times, selfish, competitive and rivalry seeking behaviours in our governments , businesses and administrations- with a more compassionate, collaborative, and more inclusive and accepting relationships- realizing more holistic and caring lives and lifestyles – cross country, cross cultural, cross working interests co-creations.

Global human and humanity development has have had as much attention as our attention for money, business or national success.

Our efforts to preserve and protect endangered life species, and to conserve[9] natural habitats in our planetary environment have been successful and have resulted in a resilient and ever available diverse, purity and richness of nature.

We have created the holding space for a global population of 9 billion people being able to enjoy – in equal, just and fair conditions- their freedoms of expressions and movement, and to allow for a life of good, happiness and meaning

Paradise on Planet Earth.

What a wonderful world that can be!

Now imagine this picture – just for a minute- and for yourself.

---

[9] say at least 30% of the original: oceans, land, foresty, water ways

What I do know- and have come to see- is that that picture of how our world best may look like over say 100 years, is today different between our nations and our people.

It depends who you are, and it depends on where you are.

If you ask this question to the one who has become eco-conscious and lives and works in eco-villages around the globe, you will receive a different painting and picture then if you ask this question to a futurist or scientist and who has come to abide, live and believe in the prospects of smart cities , new technologies and breakthrough innovations.[10]

I also know that the ones who are presently in the game of money or power- will also look with some different eyes, minds and ears to the world to come.

Some will believe that our world will continue to be on a Darwin journey- where the simple rule of the jungle will prevail: The survival of the fittest.

Over the coming years, the simple reality is, and that is true in their more pragmatic eyes, that the stronger ones will get stronger-. or may see them to weaken and fail: those that can compete or have the talent to maintain pace with the rapid developments, and those that can't.

So- in their eyes- they see the rise of (some) Paradise on Earth, best built around their ivory towers (cities and nations) of wealth, consumption, entertainment and power, and whereby some may or will be left behind, will be losers or will be part of a trickle-down economy: - due to lack of resources, development potential , attention and further justified by the competitive rivalries , lack of local talent, governance or failings in (local-) culture or leadership, etc.

It's that simple.

The present rivalries and politicking between the West (US/ OECD) with e.g. China, Russia and with India, Africa and the rest and so on- tells a little of what and how this painting can be.

Ask multi-national corporate leaders what they expect to see over 100 years, and they will paint you a picture of a global community that has ever become more wealthy and rich and diverse in population- with a continued and healthy demand and appetite for food, water, energy, housing, consuming goods, travel, education, health, entertainment, etc. etc.

Basically the UN Sustainable Development goals.

Of course they will come to speak about competition, but they will also dream with you about free trade and how a new world order can be created whereby their

---

[10] , such as Artifical Intelligence, Augmented Reality, Big-Data Computing, Robotification, Bio-engineering, Quant-computing, Gen modifications, and so on.

corporate become the instrument and the co-facilitators that develop the global and local talents, communities and platform delivery capabilities that can bring about and connect (sustainable) consuming demands with production capacities and in a new, better, more sustainable way.[11]

More and more harmonic. More and more collaborative. More and more social inclusive and sustainable with planet Earth.

Business a Force of Good.

Ask a concerned politician in the West, and who is aware of its' colonial past and present sentiments in some of the UN, you may hear:

We will see a thriving global community of 9 billion people, and whereby the white men (the 1 billion of the previous rich west) is sitting on a little bench in the corner

Finally- but not in the least- there is the school of thought around- and that is the school of spirituality, religion and human conscious.

Those are the people that resonate and understand Pope Francis call Laudato Si (Spirit of Assisi)- and these people can be found in all shapes and forms (in all religions, new age) around the globe.

Truly inspirational.

In their view- our journey into our future- is simply best served if we are to re-gain our balance and interest for a more inspired world:

A world where human and natural development receive the right form of dignity, respect, priority and attention[12]- and are in better position and balance with the present demanding needs of state, economies and societies.

A world of spirituality and loving kindness.

Ask these people how they dream the world over 100 years to be- and you may hear dignified responses and hopes, such as:

A world where we have created Peace and All Good for humanity, beyond any sufferings.

A world where human and humanity have re-found their rightful place back in Creation, being true, congruent, and in compassion - and better stewards of Creation and our Common Home.

---

[11] Better Business-Better World of the Business and Sustainable Development Commission
[12] Compassionate, loving kindness, caring

A world where religion (and/or spirituality) and religious guidance (calm) has helped to achieve Global Peace[13] and Harmony, and a world where religion (spirituality) has gained the place back into the hearts and minds of our people : in our businesses, in our national economies and in our state- and societal-governance models.[14]

A world where Adam and Eve have found a way to redeem their sins, Christ Love has been received and people see God for who and what he is.

As I have walked on this journey now quite some while, I must admit- that where-ever I have posed this question, I have always been pleasantly surprised about the richness and creativity of our (individual and group) imaginations on how our world[15] may look like over 100 years.[16]

Over this time, and I again - I have to admit- I have come to see and acknowledge the power of such individual or more group-shared *dreams* (or *inspiration*).

Some people have come to believe that it is only by our dream[17], by our imagination, that we will and are to be able to move, change or create in our world:

The simple logic used:

If you cannot imagine it- it cannot be created

If it can be imagined- it may be able to come about.[18]

So- it may well be that by internalizing our dreams[19] from our unconscious into our conscious and collective– that we are and may become the creators of our future.

As such- our future can be shaped and build, and our *shared* future, in essence, is dependent and will be based on the collective of our dreams[20], decisions, and creations going forwards.

---

[13] The CEFID. Inter-religious peace-building dialogue initiative from the St. Francis' Friars Minor Conventional Order in Assisi- and which started with the first inter-religious global day of peace prayer celebrated and hosted by St. Pope John Paul II in 1986.

[14] E.g. listen to the very wise words and words of inspiration of Cardinal Pietro Parolin at WEF Davos 2017

[15] Or Country, company, community

[16] Let me be clear here: for this conversation and booklet I believe we donot need to be exact, comprehensive or exhaustive on the type of scenario's or dreams we may see, recognize and collectively share. That is not the point of this conversation. The point and intent of this small booklet is to get ourselves on the journey of discovery: in conversation and in conversion!

[17] [17] meditation, prayer, contemplation, communion with the Divine

[18] meditation, prayer, contemplation, communion with the Divine.

[19] Individual or group

[20] Star on the Horizon

Now – and as I moved around, and asked these questions in classroom workshops and in professional business meetings and events, - and as I am a little curious man- I have asked the same question a little different:

How long will it take us to get this dream about in our world ?

And let me start with an answer I received from a very kind St Francis Friar minor , here in Assisi:

At least another 800 years.

And that is quite a telling answer.

Let me try to explain:

It was about 800 years ago that St Francis received his inspiration and his new views, dreams and eyes on the world:

To make the world more just, fair, socially inclusive and caring for Creation.

Basically – the dream we wish to discuss and materialize for our next 30 or 100 years.

Now- the fact that a *deep* religious practicing friar, and who listens regularly to personal confessions from people from all over the world, tells me that "Peace and All Good" will take our human civilisation at least another 800 years to achieve- may make you agree with me two things:

Sense of Urgency

Sense of Calm

Let me explain again:

We may see and read in the reply and response of this most kind friar that his present appraisal of "the situation we are in" – may not be to our liking.

We may feel that our present times asks and invites us to be and become and do much better:

To better help the organisation and materialization of this better dream world.

We may become inspired and enthused- and by attuning ourselves to the following statement:

We can do better. Together, we can build the world we want.

But in the answer of the Friar is also some peaceful, and something of quiet:

Again two small messages I can see:

The good news is that humanity is (supposedly) still to exist over 800 years, and that *our patience in our dream* helps us to see that we are only to achieve small stepping stones of "Peace and All Good" in our lives- to become member and partner on the journey we see ourselves in:

To bring Heaven (make Paradise) on Earth.

Our world future nor our dream does not ask us to do and achieve the super-humane: it simply invites us to step onto the journey (of conversion) and become truly and whole part of the solution.

Not the problem.

But let me share you here a couple of other views and perspective on our question of time (and timing)

Let me remind you (first) that the UN Sustainable Development goals and agenda has been agreed[21] at the UN in September 2015 in New York, and that the 195 country members have (of course) all set (a different course) of national and political/economic agenda and development maturities and paths.

Now – as I have come to ask the question in different forum of Energy professionals, defence specialists and country (sustainable) development experts- and I would like to share you briefly the following views, responses, and perhaps serving as a wake-up call:

In conversation with a most senior representative of a multi-national energy company, I received the following answer:

If we do not find the ways to agree our better pathways forwards on Energy and UN Sustainable development over the coming 5 years- individually and collectively- we will surely see ourselves into a major planetary and humanitarian crisis.

The simple reasoning applied by this senior in the oil and gas industry:

We cannot attain sustainable societies or the sustainable development goals , if we do not know how to attain sustainable, affordable and available Energy to All.

And we presently don't.

We cannot *power* ourselves into sustainable societies, if the foundations, the roots of these societies are based on un-sustainable energy production and consumption patterns.'

We presently do.[22]

---

[21] Voluntary national program, goals and commitments
[22] energyandstuff.org - back to the future of economics

And we may *all* also sense and feel:

We desperately need to attain the (UN) Sustainable Development Goals if we aspire to achieve (global, regional and local) living conditions and societies that can be free of conflict, (old or new) terrorism and wars.

In conversation with a senior consultant on national defence, intelligence and energy and resources- I did hear the following:

If nothing changes in the present trends of our geo-politics of emotions - all seem to indicate that we are to see a major resource or climate change crisis, conflict or war before mid-century.

Whilst the UN Sustainable development goals asks and invites member countries to consider clean energy and the appropriate programs and actions on climate change before 2030, the realities today, and if you ask key resource holding countries, companies and operators in this arena- you will and may hear and meet with the following voices and opinions:

It will take at least the coming century to move from our present fossil fuel based economies towards renewable energy architectures and sustainable economies.[23]

Gas and Oil will be the fuels of the future and that will last. Gas is the bridging future to our energy future. The lobbies and working interests to do so are clear.

Not to bore you- but today's reality is that we have crossed 24 planetary boundaries[24] in our natural and socio-economic configuration between ourselves, our human civilisation and our nature.

So- it's not only Climate Change.

It's actually lot's more.

Our global energy industries and intensified economies are surely contributors in this game.

And with the present trends and practices on-going (of an ever growing and expanding global and national economies)- and in line with Pope Francis observations in Laudato Si- we may agree that this better not continue.

Not in the coming 5, 15 or 30 years.

Something has to change. Something has to converse.

That is what this inspiration is about.

---

[23] E.g. BP (or Exxon Mobile) World Energy Outlooks 2017
[24] E.g. 2015 Research from the Stockholm Resilience Centre: Fresh waterways, fishery, forests, oceans, nitrogen cycle, climate, chemicals in nature, bio-diversity, etc.,

Whilst we may have another 800 years to go before we may see ourselves living in "Paradise on Planet Earth", we *know* that we have only the coming 30- 100 years to solve some of our today's sources for conflicts, some of our behaviours and attitudes in and between ourselves, and some of our established[25] ways of human, economic, technology and ecology development.

And we may even sense, feel and know that some of those issues are best solved in the coming decades (5-15 years), if we want to give our children and children's children a chance of having hope, meaning and the ever progressive experiences, consciences and dreams of a socially just, inclusive and better shared world.

Together with you I am inspired and excited.

I am excited that together we are and can walk on this path of Beauty, Hope and More Wonder.

I am inspired to see how we can make use of the seldom wise and inspirational words of Pope Francis (Laudato Si) and that we can discuss and bring forth and about "his views and tone of voice" in our modernized world of business, economy and administration, and international relationships..

With you – as I hope- we may believe that the better changes can come about if we allow and make ourselves available for this call of conversion.

Conversion in Ourselves. Convergence between Ourselves.Conversion in our Leadership styles- the way we work, live, breath and bring change about.

And

Conversion of the organisational forms and formats by which we aim to attain sustainable development and sustainable societies.

I call this my St Francis 2.0

Our conversion is the path whereby we learn to walk in calm, but where we *never ever* keep our eyes and ears off the Star on our Horizon:

One people. One planet. and

Living In the Spirit of Assisi (Laudato Si):

May God Bless you all.

1. Peace and All Good

2. Unity in Diversity

3. Listening, dialogue, mediation and understanding: **building common groud (convergence)**

---

[25] Shadow sides

Chapter 1: Challenges in our Leadership

From Empire Era to Planetary Consciousness conversion on a Global Scale

Without too many words- we can look at our human civilisation as an evolutionary path over time.

Thousands, Tens of Thousands, Millions of year.

I invite you to read some of the texts in the Appendix - to familiarize yourself with the more scientific and anthropological views on our cultural and human development.

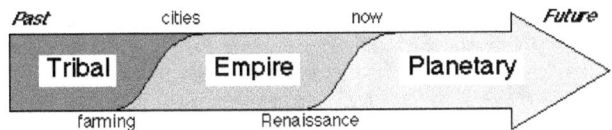

Earlier this year, the key geological institute and scientists declared that we have entered into the world of the anthropocene.[26]

Add to that, that today, as in all times - we live in quite interesting times.

Our world is seemingly experiencing an acceleration of civilization and with some quite dynamic changes.

In our geo-politics of emotions, in our demographies and economies, in and through our sciences and new technologies, through innovation and through social- changes including our relationships with the natural environment.

A recent report by the OECD concluded that *never ever* have we been so successful in raising people out of poverty and make them member of a new global middle-class.[27]

As such, we can see our world as being under rapid construction and development, with new cities, new wealth and wealth distribution being created, every day, and in an unprecedented speed.

---

24 <u>Human Impact has pushed the Earth into the Anthropocene, Scientists say</u>
[27] Words from Erik Solheim, SG UNEP

Never ever before were we so capable. Never ever before were we also so capable to destroy something or compete.

Over the coming two to three decades some 3 billion people in Asia, Middle-East & Africa, Latin-America are expected to join the new global middle-class and are prognosed to enjoy the same consumption patterns, the same living comforts in their homes, in their offices and in their transportation now so much taken for granted in the OECD and upper middle class families in the emerging and developing nations.[1] By the mid of the century, we expect we will be living with 9 billion people- sharing one planet.

Our global economy is expected to rise from 90 trillion USD GDP (today) till at least 180-210 trillion USD by year 2050, if nothing dramatically changes.

This may entail a steep rise in the use of our Earth natural resources[28] and a further crossing and erosion of some of our planetary boundaries (which allows for a shared living with Creation).

Right now, 1.2 billion people are living in extreme poverty beyond and without proper access to food, water, housing, health, education, etc. For millions, night-time brings darkness or the dim lighting of a kerosene lantern or candle. In Africa, these challenges disproportionately affect those living in rural areas. In Africa, over 290 million people use kerosene as their main source of lighting. Even for those living with access to electricity, this is often insufficient or unreliable.

When we have energy- we can see human development, including the abilities for water, food, health, education, jobs and comfortable living standards. Energy is the physical stuff that makes things possible.

The role business and government leadership can play over this opportunity and the more integrated stewardship over human development in balance with society, economy and nature- has only recently been recognized, and particular thanks to the words of Pope Francis Encyclical Laudato Si and the acceptance of the UN Sustainable Development Goals for 2030.

The year 2015 saw the end of the Millennium Development Goals and the establishment of the Sustainable Development Goals, with a real focus on a more holistic and integral human development, in balance with his or her natural environment.

Over the coming decades we have an extraordinary opportunity to re-write some of our present beliefs, rules and experiences. We can iron-out some of the inequalities in power, inequalities in communication and understandings, some of our sources of conflict, some of our unhealthy and unsustainable practices in our present industrial and trade relations system.

---

[28] **UNEP Global Material Resource Exploitation and Use** from **Energy for One World**

Or we do not, and as a result, we may see ourselves in some serious new trouble.

Government and Business Leadership are essential in our quest to create more peaceful, calm and vibrant sustainable societies- to all.

Hence, getting this right is of vital importance.

Not only for our own Nation and Business, but also in a wider context.

Phrased a little different:

So how are we going to do this: Having only One planet to share and ideally staying out of trouble?[29]

Well- that is the quest of this dialogue and conversation.

---

[29] This boooklet is mostly occupied with the present Style and Tones of Voices in our present day Leadership. A review of the present functioning of the international order and organizations such as UN, ADB, World Bank, IMF, IEA, OPEC, UN SDSN, etc. has been carried our separately, but does not form part of this brief.

Resource exploitation and sharing with 9 billion people

Let's get down to business.

And let's do some straight talk on our aims for Sustainable Development of our Global Village.

And let's start with some most recent words from our world most re-knowned expert in this field: Prof. Jeffrey Sachs- from Columbia University, and the UN SDSD network:

By Jeffrey Sachs   JULY 19, 2016

AROUND THE WORLD, people are calling for a new kind of globalization. The current version, once called the Washington Consensus, has delivered economic growth but at enormous cost: rising inequalities of income, massive environmental destruction, and growing lawlessness. The search is on for a new approach, sometimes called sustainable development, to ensure that economic growth is also socially just and environmentally sustainable.

Nine months ago, Pope Francis spoke to world leaders at the United Nations calling for such a holistic and moral vision, and the world leaders responded by adopting a new framework of cooperation for the years 2016-2030, called Sustainable Development Goals, or SDGs. The SDGs were negotiated over several years based on a simple yet powerful idea: Every one of the 193 UN member countries can benefit by a globalization that combines economic, social, and environmental objectives.

The aim is not global governance but global decency. The responsibility for change still rests with national governments and local communities. Economic development still counts, but alongside social fairness and environmental sustainability. Yet all nations can benefit from a common global framework and the efforts of every other country to achieve it.

Americans could be among the world's biggest beneficiaries of the new Sustainable Development Goals, though the concept has hardly been discussed in the American media. While other countries have been holding forums to discuss the SDGs, the United States has largely ignored them except on campuses, in some city governments, and in many companies. Yet this is a case where the United States has a lot to learn, and benefit, from other countries.

The SDGs work for the United States because they address the core problems that ail our society. Since 1980, America has become much richer, with national income per person up by 80 percent. Yet America is now vastly more divided between rich and poor; more vulnerable to droughts, floods, and extreme storms; and less confident in its future. An astounding 73 percent of Americans believe that the country is "on the wrong track." In short, America has become much richer but much less fair and environmentally sustainable.

The Sustainable Development Goals pour scorn on the once-popular idea that "greed is good" by emphasizing that an American society (indeed any society) built to last must look beyond greed to honesty, solidarity, and sustainability. And the SDGs offer up some practical benchmarks to measure progress. The implications for the United States are eye-opening.

While all countries have a ways to go to achieve sustainable development, the United States has much farther to go than many other countries. Each country's state of sustainable development can be scored on a set of detailed indicators measuring poverty, nutrition, health care, education, income, jobs, gender equality, gaps of rich and poor, environmental pollution, and other specific standards for the 17 SDGs. I recently participated in the first-ever such effort to measure global progress toward the SDGs by producing an SDG Index that covers 149 countries and 77 indicators (available at www.sdgindex.org on Wednesday).

According to the new SDG Index, the United States ranks 25th in the world in the progress toward the SDGs, far ahead of the world's poorest countries but also far behind the world leaders. The world leaders in sustainable development are the Scandinavian countries: Sweden, Denmark, and Norway, ranking first, second, and third, respectively. Northern European countries account for the remaining top 10. Canada also far outpaces the United States, ranking 13th, and Australia ranks 20th.

The SDG rankings reflect deep and instructive differences between the United States and the SDG leaders in how our societies tick and the quality of life that we enjoy. The Scandinavian economies (and Northern European countries generally) have much lower maternal and infant death rates, higher life expectancy, longer vacation times, and a far lower inequality of income. Sweden's homicide rate is around one-seventh of America's and its incarceration rate is roughly one-tenth. Compared with Americans the countries leading in sustainable development are also happier, with much higher ratings of self-assessed "life satisfaction."

Even the world's SDG-leading countries have their work cut out for them in order to achieve sustainable development. In order to stop human-caused climate change, for example, every high-income country has yet to shift energy production from fossil fuels (coal, oil, and gas) to low-carbon renewables (such as solar and wind). Two of the Sustainable Development Goals call for the shift to low-carbon energy, and the SDG Index will help to track that progress country by country in future years.

What makes the SDGs especially important is that they are far more than just another political concept or utopian ideal. They are specific, time-bound goals (to the year 2030) that have been agreed to by every UN member state, including the United States. Of course, international agreements don't guarantee international action, yet the SDGs offer at least the chance for a global-scale effort to set things in a better direction. They respond to Pope Francis' call in his encyclical Laudato si' "to think of one world with a common plan."

This week at the United Nations, 22 governments are presenting to the world their initial efforts to achieve the SDGs. The United States, no surprise, is not among these first 22 countries. We are understandably absorbed in, and distracted by, the presidential campaign.

Yet despite the current distractions, let's work toward the United States sharing the SDG stage at the UN in one year's time, when the SDGs will once again be No

beyond short-term politics, to the very question of our national objectives and our cohesion as a society. As the rest of the world is recognizing at the highest levels of religion, politics, business, and civil society, the concept of sustainable development offers us the chance to put the world on a more prosperous, fair, and sustainable path.

No matter who is elected in November, America will still be on the wrong track and in need of a change of direction. - Jeffrey D. Sachs is director of the Earth Institute at Columbia University and author of "The Age of Sustainable Development."

And it's not difficult to read in these words some more serious forms of concerns and dis-appointments (if not total dis-illusion).

Some dis-appointment that the United States is - as of yet- not seriously partaking in a serious analysis, reflection, dialogue and organisation to the attainment of the sustainable development goals within its'own national borders, in its trade relations and beyond.

And concerns with the present Presidential Elections and Campaigns- how seldom the dialogue and attention is for the re-direction of the American economy towards a more and better sustainable pathways.[30]

As this is actually quite urgent and important-

Let me explain:

Well- first of all, and Professor Sachs knows this as no other, it is the USA who has taken traditionally the lead in progressing integrated UN Programs into our global community. Without any commitments from the USA, global programs such as UN SDGs are bound to fail.

Best to explain this with a report. A detailed one.

UNEP Global Material Resource Exploitation and Use from **Energy for One World**

---

[30] These words were written before President Trump took office in January 2017

Now I understand that you may not be reading this full report, but the message and contents of this report is actually quite simple and the details are actually quite unique, quite revealing and quite concerning.

In some very simple terms, the report is stating that over the last 40 years, our global village has tripled (!) the commodity resource exploitation from mother Earth.

Three times more resource commodity exploitation today - *every day*- than 40 years ago.

That is a lot.

That is actually highly unsustainable.

Now the trend going forwards, and if nothing changes, will be again a two- or three fold increase of additional Earth resource exploitation.

Doubling or tripling of what we are doing today.

How unsustainable do you want us to become?

What will happen to the affordability and availability of these resources?

Will we see ourselves compete- or do you expect us to share, equitably and fairly?

Do you think that this is attuned enough to the needs for 5- 7 generations of humanity? Our children's children and so forth.

This should alarm you.

Now comes some other news.

And you may read in this - some good news, and some bad news.

A recent report by the OECD concluded that *never ever* have we been so successful in raising people out of poverty and make them member of a new global middle-class.

In fact, and again as per current prognosis, over the coming two to three decades we are to expect to raise another 2-3 billion people from near poverty into consuming middle-class.

And that is surely some very good news for those people affected. And for those that care.[31]

OECD Sustainable Development Business and Finance 2016 highlights booklet final from **Energy for One World**

---

[31] See also Erik Solheim Editorial and words of guidance – in the separate table, attached.

But it is highly concerning - if you consider that the aggregate of our human consumption patterns are exploiting the resources of mother Earth, including unsettling of what is left of untouched Nature (remember Pope Francis Laudato Si's and his call for care for our common Home and Creation?).

And now comes some thinking:

The present American Dream, with unconstrained economic growth (for corporates and consumers), its' material consuming patterns, the energy and resource material use, the eco-footprint, and the export of these behaviours in the international trade relations is unsustainable, and harms us.

It is not only America that we are to be concerned with. It is in China, in India, it is factual everywhere around the globe:'

Our present economic model, the pace, and our overseas trade and expansion strategies- are not sustainable.

Full stop.

Our insatiable hunger for material goods, production and consumption, jobs and economic growth- is not helping us to steer the aggregate of our human civilisation to a more, calm, peaceful and more sustainable pathway.[32]

Also not in the North and not in the South.

Something has to change. Something has to converse.

Especially - if our today's care is to include and plan for at least another 7 generations to come.

Our children's children and so forth.

In the introduction of earlier mentioned OECD report, George Soros gave some words and considerations to this need to change and converse- in our business ways and international business relations:

---

[32] See also e.g. the story of energy and stuff, prepared by some senior ex-Shell Group Executives

Let' listen to some of his words. and I quote:

The Sustainable Development Goals (SDGs) represent an unprecedented articulation of the "public interest" at a global scale for all the peoples of the world. As such they force us to ask ourselves difficult questions about how we do business. Yes, there are countless business opportunities that could advance the self-interest of thousands of entrepreneurs and investors while also advancing the SDGs. By the same token, however, the SDGs also help us identify where we have an opportunity to better regulate and restrain the pursuit of personal profit through public policy, international agreements and stricter business norms. The articulation of the public interest in the SDGs can, in short, reveal both where self-interest aligns with the greater good, and where they conflict. The need here is to encourage private business activity where they align, and better regulate it where they conflict.

These are the true "business opportunities" that the SDGs offer. They invite us to address the question: how can those of us in business contribute to the achievement of these goals as investors, entrepreneurs and executives? All of us share the need for healthy and stable economies, fair and well-governed societies, well-regulated value chains in trade, mitigation of climate change, world peace, and respect for human rights. This volume explores how the private sector can be a powerful actor in promoting the achievement of such common aims, and where it must exercise restraint. In this respect, the public good should be both the limiting factor in encouraging those who act in their own self-interest, and the goal for those who seek to act in the collective interest of society. We must avoid not only the obvious scourge of corruption in this effort, but the danger of exploitation. We must seek to not only do more good, but also ask ourselves where we can do less harm.

Given the scale of the problems the world is facing, and the unprecedented levels of global inequality, these questions are not only important, but urgent. Business must play its part. Governments and multilateral institutions who steward resources on behalf of us all, must play their part. Regulators at local, national and international levels must play their part. Collectively we can mobilise financial resources at historic scales to implement a wide range of development efforts. But sustainable global progress cannot be achieved through monetary means and investment alone. It is vital that capacity is strengthened in individuals and in the institutions of civil society to play a vigorous part in carrying out such a transformation, including the thoughtful regulation of business activity.

I encourage anyone interested in development or business to read this report and to take to heart the challenges, and the opportunities, that it explores.

Let me phrase this in a bit simpler frame- and perhaps a little more clear:

As we raise more people out of poverty and into middle-class (in the East, the South)

and

As we raise the general standard of living and wealth and wealth aggregation in the richer and more developed parts of our world - in the Americas, in Europe, in in Asia (China, India, Far-East), Africa and Middle-East so on

and

that today,

- we have crossed 24 planetary boundaries[33] that we- collectively- may consider un-sustainable,
- Add to this our continued hunger for earth commodity and mineral resources, which tripled over the last 40 years, and if nothing changes- is prognosed to rise as we see today

we simply can observe,

- something has to change or converse- if we don't want to end-up competing and or outperform each other, but like to have 9 billion people living harmoniously together,
- with affordable, available and sustainable comfort and consuming patterns-

Something has to change especially when we opt to at least care and plan for 7 generations of humanity. Our children's children and so forth.

Something more and better than we see ourselves organized doing today (with the UN Sustainable Development Goals).

Yes- Jeffrey Sachs' article and words are *telling.*

Yes- our alarm bells may go off.

and

Yes- we may start to have some better dialogues and more intense conversations how we can organize and steer our mainstream national economies and our

---

[33] Stockholm resilience centre. **Great Acceleration 2015** from **International Geosphere-Biosphere Programme**

mother ship Earth and human civilisation into a more healthier and more positive pathway.

Today, you may be concerned with Professor Jeffrey Sachs, as we progress and see ourselves doing business, expanding our corporate footprints, building cities, industries and infrastructures in the South-South and North-South axis of development., no matter what innovation or resource efficiency advocates and made believes may foretell.

Pope Francis *saw* right. Jeffrey Sachs *call* is right.

Laudato Si (his encyclical) could not have been written in a better moment of our human development time.

Word for Word.

Let us open our eyes, and help each of us to see and do what may make some very good common sense.

Let us see ourselves some better ways, better times, and better lives.

Let us agree to see how to navigate and re-direct our shared common ways.

Development Co-operation Report 2016:The Sustainable Development Goals as Business Opportunities (Report)[34]

by Erik Solheim, Chair of the OECD Development Assistance Committee

In 2015, when world leaders adopted the Sustainable Development Goals, we committed to the most inclusive, diverse and comprehensive and ambitious development agenda ever. By doing so, we acknowledged that development challenges are global challenges. The new global goals represent a universal agenda, applying equally to all countries in the world.

The year 2015 was the best in history for many people. We are taller, and better nourished and educated than ever. We live longer. There is less violence than at any other point in history. Over the past decades many countries, spearheaded by the Asian "miracles" – such as in Korea, the People's Republic of China and Singapore – have had enormous development success. By believing in the market and the private sector, these nations have experienced strong economic growth and several hundred million people have been brought out of poverty. The debate within the development community on the importance of markets and the private sector is a thing of the past. The debate is won.

But based on astonishing success, we need to bring everyone on board. The 2030 aim is to eradicate extreme poverty, but to do it in an environmentally sustainable way. Luckily – for the first time in history – humanity has the capacity, knowledge and resources needed to achieve this. Never before was this the case. The leaders of the past have never set such goals, nor did they have at their disposal the policies and the resources to reach them. The Sustainable Development Goals cover the economic, social and environmental dimensions of life. And they emphasise that increased co-operation between the public and the private sector is vital to reach them.

Implementing the new Sustainable Development Goals will require all hands on deck, working in concert to build on each other's strengths. In this report we look at the opportunities for businesses both to make money and do good for people and the environment. We must go beyond traditional thinking that business revenues depend on destroying the environment. Smart investment in sustainable development is not charity – it is good business and it opens up opportunities.

In developing countries, small and medium enterprises are considered the engine of growth. In Asia, they make up to 98% of all enterprises and employ 66% of the workforce. Especially for green growth, small and medium businesses can play an important role by acting as suppliers of and investors in affordable and local green technologies. For instance, in Africa several businesses offer "pay-as-you-go" solar energy to low-income households that do not have access to central resources.

---

[34] Another good reference in this frame is the booklet Better Business- better World from the Business and Sustainable development commission

Over the next 15 years, billions of dollars will be invested annually by the public and private sectors. We need to make sure that this money creates jobs, boosts productive capacity and enables local firms to access new international markets in a sustainable way. What's more, these flows are often coupled with transfer of technology that has positive and long-term effects.

This report cites the results of interviews with executives from 40 companies that had performed above the industry average in terms of both financial and sustainability-performance metrics in various sectors – including oil and mining, gym shoes, soup, cosmetics and telecommunications. The research demonstrates that sustainable action can contribute to increased efficiency and profits, gains above and beyond their social and environmental benefits. The returns on capital include reduced risk, market and portfolio diversification, increased revenue, reduced costs, and improved products.

We need to take these experiences further. The 17 Sustainable Development Goals represent a pipeline of sustainable investment opportunities for responsible business. But fulfilling that potential will mean ensuring that business does good – for people and the planet – while doing well economically.

Although some countries are making progress, no country has achieved environmental sustainability. The worse things get, the more difficult it will be to find solutions. We need to take action now. There is more bang for every buck when profits are combined with bringing people out of poverty, improving environmental sustainability and ensuring gender equality. For example:

Ethiopia's growth has benefited the poor and the country aims to become a middle-income country without increasing its carbon emissions.

Brazil has reduced poverty and equality while cutting deforestation by 80%.

Costa Rica has revolutionised conservation by providing cash payments for people who maintain natural resources. Forests now cover more than 50% of the country's land, compared to 21% in the 1980s.

The Indonesian rainforests, the largest in Asia, are doing much better than recently. Deforestation decreased for the first time in 2013 and the positive trend is continuing. The main palm oil companies have made a no new deforestation pledge.

Poverty reduction can be green and fair. But we need to remember that neither developing nor developed countries will sacrifice development for the environment. But development comes to a stop if natural resources are exhausted, water continues to be polluted and soils are degraded beyond manageable levels.

For those who do not benefit from all the success stories, it is necessary to identify and replicate good policies that actually improve lives. Official development assistance is important for the least developed nations and countries in conflict. Aid remains at a record high at USD 132 billion in 2015, but private investments are more than 100 times greater than aid and more important for poverty reduction and economic growth.

interventions. In this report the OECD describes how it monitors and measures the amounts being

In order to make the most of private investments for sustainable development, it is fundamental to know more about how much is being mobilised from the private sector as a result of public sector invested. The European Union found in 2014 that by blending public and private investments, EU countries used EUR 2 billion in public finance grants to mobilise around EUR 40 billion for things like constructing electricity networks, financing major road projects, and building water and sanitation infrastructure in recipient countries. We should be inspired by this example to do more. Business prospers when society prospers.

Each and every decision we take today related to private investment will have historic implications. We must learn that more and better investment is possible. Balancing economic growth with environmental sustainability is not only feasible – it is fundamental.

In this report we look at the opportunities the new Sustainable Development Goals offer for doing good business, for profits, people and the planet. It offers guidelines and practical examples of how all sectors of society can work together to deliver the 2030 Agenda. Investing in sustainable development is not charity, it is smart. We just need to go ahead and do it.

A New Balance

So- we *know* that coming decades are of importance.

We *know* that if we aspire to maintain One Planet Earth that can bear fruit for all human beings, and allow our daily labor, life, modern comforts and consuming habits,

We know that we have to make some important changes in the aggregate of our development path and established patterns of production and consumption in our global industries, economies and societies.-.[35]

It is true that the aggregate of our working and consuming behaviors in our global village is running against some serious planetary boundaries.

Climate Change not one of the least.

It is true that the industrial and chemical off-springs, emissions and pollutions in the atmosphere, water ways, and in our forests, and onto mother Earth – are having an effect on Nature, and on the conditions of our own living comfort[36] and being here.

It is true that we are knowingly over-exploiting minerals, commodities an natural resource base from mother Earth, and are (rapidly) depleting the easy-to-delve[37] resource reserves.

It is true that the amount of biodiversity is reducing- right as I write you these words- and not only from an evolutionary point of view, but also due to the impact and footprints humanity has taken in the natural environment.[38]

It is true that with the rise and development of new and intense forms of science and engineering- we cross and blur of what was formerly Life (or Nature) and

---

[35] The UN Sustainable Development goals have been designed and defined with some very good reasons, one of them- being:

[36] City pollutions: breathing, drinking water, sewage systems, etc.

[37] Cost and energy intensity of exploitation. We are rapidly running-up the creaming curve of natural resource extraction- making it every year - more costly, more energy intense and more difficult- to find and exploit the same volumes or bigger, as we are doing today. The easy stuff has been consumed over the last century. We are now entering the phase of the more complex Earth Resource Reserve bases that we are planning to consume. More complex, means also more intense methods of extraction: more chemicals, deeper, intenser and with more impact and damage to nature.

[38] Anthropocene

what is today artificially maintained or boosted with new technologies in productivities[39].

It is true that with the rise of wealth and wealthy consuming behaviors in the East and in the West, the North and in the South- and the more interconnectivity of people, cultures and information sources- *the globalization*- we can see and experience both a new global elite that seeks to live, work and act – in and from "peace and happiness" ,

But is also true that we see due to this new globalization also the rise of fear, competitions, nationalism, fundamentalism, terrorism, populism, nationalism and anti-globalisation movements.- at times at the bottom of the pyramid, the ones without a voice or so much to fear.

Of course, and as I write you these words, I know with you- that many professionals and in the various industry blood groups and sectors have become aware, competent and responsible actors in and on the above complexities-

Of course, and as I write you these words- I am aware that for all of the above, individually and in aggregate- we have now international science, research and (oversight) working committees, sector committees, government committees and so on.

Some at UN Level, some at multi-national ministerial and corporate/sectorial[40] level, and some – of course – at national and research institute level.

We have institutionalized these challenges and global (globalization) problems.[41][42]

And of course, I know with you.- that we have seen over the last 10-20 years a massive rise and diversity of organizational change and program innovations and initiatives [43][44]– and with the sole goals and focus to alleviate some , if not all of the above: to allow ourselves to stay out of trouble. To build social and communities resilience.

---

[39] Agriculture, Farming, Feeding, Breeding Cattle, Even cloning Cows (Tijanjin, China) and maybe human life. The interaction between birth and gen control, computer and human life is also where we see scientists cross new borders

[40] In Energy: e.g. IEF

[41] We would benefit if we could see the better linkages between the macro with the micro-scale in our human development

[42] E.g. talking heads at WEF Davos- over 44 years of discussions to see our world in a better place, and yet again, this year , at Davos 2017 – so painstaikingly evident – without the right formula's for change. Christine Lagarde and Larry Summers at Davos

[43] E.g. UN FCCC- Paris Climate Change Agreement

[44] Whoever has still an overview of what is happening here, on a global scale.

The UN Sustainable Development Agenda and Goals – an example in time.

Unfortunately, today's trends are not helping us.

And that is a fact.

Our material-intense wealth and consumption patterns keeps on rising, faster than we resolve.[45]

The amount of Earth resources we consume- is growing, nevertheless our resource efficiency and material waste recycling efforts[46]

The amount of pollution and damage control seems to run behind the growth curve, and can hardly keep-up with what is real and out there.

 Now- the above- would have been enough- to keep some industrial and national leadership awake- and with the simple question:

How are we going to do this?

How are we going to bend our trend, or how are we going to keep our house in order.

Keeping earth resources available, affordable and sustainable?

For the generation to come. But also for their generations and generations to come.

For the next 100- 200 years?

---

[45] UNEP Resource Report
[46] UNEP Resource Report

The Paris Climate Change Agreement and Pandora's Box

I cannot state it differently.

The attainment of the Paris Climate Change agreement, and after more than 21 (if not 40 years) of international negotiations, and at times- quite political- is and has been truly *a Game-changer*.

Never ever before came so many Country Heads together, and to collectively endorse their leading ministers and negotiators to agree on a deal.

The importance of this Agreement, and the good example this may bring to our global village in *how to manage, agree and resolve* a complex global (pollution)[47] problems- can nor may not be underestimated.

It is or to exceed Kyoto Protocol.

The Paris Climate Change Agreement, is,

-   And no matter how good or how bad you like the reading of the agreement, and the arrangements in the ways of how to go about it--

is and has become today, the present de-facto organizational structure and legal standard by *which and how* our international community can work and agree.[48]

For years to come by.

And all Parties to the agreement *may* know :

The agreement is (still) rather weak.[49]

Our "duty of care", our readiness and preparedness to help, to support and to contribute to make the Paris Climate Agreement an outstanding success in and between ourselves- has never been in history of human mankind- so important.

The Paris Climate Agreement is best to succeed. Not to fail.

---

[47] Or Resource!

[48] If we donot come to agree or add an alternative- supplementary way. (such as this proposal)

[49] Weaker then Kyoto. But more extensive in scope.

But how easy is the Agreement to succeed if today the climate realities are already seemingly beyond its' ambition levels – let alone what is required to change?[50][51]

If you like to read some concerning news on this ("the actual situation") - and from a scientific perspective (NASA)- I suggest you read the following article on actual global warming today:

Nasa: Earth is warming at a pace 'unprecedented in 1,000 years'

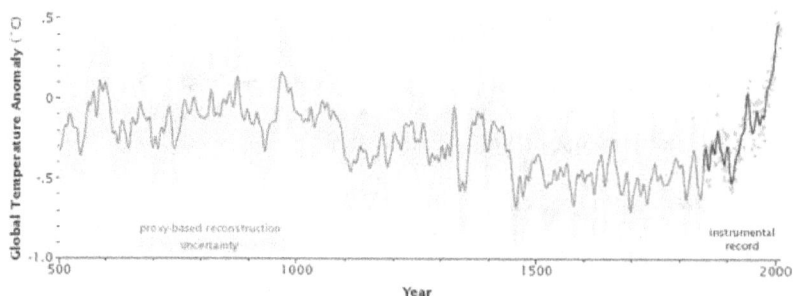

Let me assure you- further:

The amount of political opportunism in and between the Parties to the Agreement is and has been quite visible for all to see and available.

Self-interests, and political opportunism[52] has seen here some very good company with the more altruistic side of the Parties.

The (political an industry sector) lobby, political status[53] and demands for funds, finance and compensations has been rivaling here with the more honest and courageous attempts of truly bending and mending the aggregate and international course and saving Humanity from unnecessary suffering [54]and our Planet Earth (Humanity)

The Good, the Bad and the Ugly all intertwined.

---

[50] A turning point is needed for electricity and climate
[51] California is about to find out what a truly radical climate policy looks like
[52] In the public eye: western political leadership felt inspired and were expected by their public eye (and Climate Change Pressure Groups) to see an International Agreement. Very generally speaking- Eastern and Emerging Nations were to see to be good negotiators and assure national economic growth interests – also with respect to historic obligations and responsibilities from the West.
[53] Being seen as a VIP: "urgent and important"
[54] Especially the poor and deprived. And the countries that will be most effected by climate change.

All around.

So- the success of the Paris Climate Change agreement is in our abilities to organize beyond some of its' walls – and beyond some of its' ugliness- into a success.

A true success

And that is not simple.

As the actual litmus test of the effects of the agreement can only be seen or measured over a period of 10, 20 or even 30 years.

As the root of its' organization is and has been from the environmental lobby and scientific community, we have to agree- this is not necessarily where todays' power and economics are "at play".

As the root of its' organization- which is scientific - is also to seek ever year new funds, for ever more research on ever new technologies and innovation dreams.

The Paris Climate Agreement, under the UN FCCC- and it ministerial corps diplomats- is not in the "heart of hearts" from those that actually lead or have the experience with the energy or country economic sectors.[55]

Hence, the organizational forms and the processes in the UN FCCC scientific and management committees and conferences does not spell for its ease of implementation or direct ways of execution (other than to be a mechanism of research, policy and (investment) funds). [56]

Of translation from paper into true worldly actions.

So far, it has been extremely slow and cumbersome to agree and to deliver.[57]

Let us all agree on that.

Well there is – of course- some good news.

We can truly celebrate the agreement, and we can celebrate some momentum in the accumulation of goodwill, intent and finance[58] – for the realization of some of the agreement.

---

[55] President Trump, Rex Tillerson and the new cabinet of the new US administration let here no doubt.
[56] Its an umbrella organization- and dependent on state and economic actors to execute and deliver.
[57] Remember Prof. Jeffrey Sachs observations on e.g. full SDGs.
[58] From Western governments, corporate elites and finance power houses.

It has been US leadership, in essence President Obama, that has recognized and seen that the actual uphold of the Paris Climate Change Agreement can (also) be secured as part of a more on-going conversation in and between a fewer number of economies and nations.

The "Big League".

G2 and G20.

Between China, US – or the G20- so to speak.

And that is where some of our true hopes may be.[59]

It is if the US Leadership- with China and India - will find the more harmonic and balanced ways – in and between themselves- to uphold each other to its' form.

But the Chinese and Indian Leadership has been operating rather careful on the issue of Climate Change[60], and – in the present international arena- *know very well* how to stay out of the spot-light, and how to use befriended states to make the more assertive arguments. [61] [62]

In essence, the Paris Climate Agreement- may and can also become "a new can of worms":

A new "South China Sea"

Everybody knows that no sovereign nation, today and so far, likes to be told by others or the global community- what or how to consume.

And that is now exactly where the art of the maintenance of this deal is.

Everybody in the room finds it easy to tell the other what to do.

---

[59] With President Trump, Rex Tillerson and the new cabinet of the new US administration we may be here in doubt

[60] Chinese and Indian Leadership has maintained their views that the origins of the Climate Change Problem situates in the West. It is the West that needs to clean-up their acts, and pay compensations and support the others with new technologies and infrastructure. China's commitments under the agreement- are only a matter of good will (and of course a gesture to the Chinese Public to clean-up the air in cities: environment and breathing problems!)

[61] Both President Xi and PM Modi, however, have made a public commitment to act. Also in National and Public Speeches. But is this truly Top of Mind, also of our other world leaders?

[62] Perhaps also a little wait-and-see what the Presidential Election in the US is going to bring: A Republican President Trump?

Everybody in the room finds it more difficult to change own national working habits and ways,- in own country, interests or needs- and in and in order to make room and give allowance to the other- and the overall.

So- whilst the Paris Climate Change agreement is a litmus test in our global community- in how civilized and committed we are - and will be able to execute a complex distribution and resource allocation situation (or pollution problem),

The reality today is:

We don't know.

We don't know what the political process and the government, financial-economic development in the USA (or the West) allows or can let the agreement to proceed,[63][64]

We don't know if the commitments in the finance-energy sector are strong enough to bend course[65]

We don't know if the Agreement is, can or will become actually an instrument in the hands of geo-politics of emotions and new political opportunism.

From the East as well in the West. From the North to the South.

We don't know – in 5 or 10 years from now- and in "the game of thrones" being played between China and USA- what the nature of the conversations- and the international sentiments and emotions- will be under the agreement.[66]

What the intents have been at the table in Paris. Or what the intents are now perceived to be.

We don' t know if the cry and call for finance and (historic) compensation becomes and gets the overhand , over and above in maintaining and building true humanitarian progress, true change, and a true cleaner planet.

We don't' know if national governments or business administration are actually able and capable to change course, and re-direct their energy sector and

---

[63] Liabilities, Compensation, capacity building, technology transfers to the emerging nations, plus rapid change of own energy mix and infrastructures. Dependent on Economic Costs, Political and Business Elite will an abilities to deliver beyond own national government agreement and agenda.

[64] President Duterte of Phillipines recent commentary in internaitonal newspaper not helpful, July 2016

[65] Today- they are not. The key boardrooms of all major oil and gas companies around the globe donot show a willingness to change course.

[66] A planet more hotter, flatter and ever more crowded : consuming people who are middle-class

footprints (e.g. continued exploitation of oil and gas) and our energy intense consuming patters the other ways.

We don't know how the Parties will behave when the times get a little more tough, or a little more rough- for real[67].

We don't know.

And the fact that we don't know- should concern you.

Something else may concern, as well..

"Cleaning-up" the first 15-25 % of the energy mix in any country or region (change from fossil fuels to wind, solar) is today easy.

But it is the costs, true efforts, capabilities and actual technological and economic transformations required - to clean-up an present energy mix beyond 30% renewable- that should worry us.[68]

That is today's (engineering and capabilities) reality.

Our present petro-energy intense industries, transportation, consuming habits and economies are today "not fit" to run on 100% renewables only.

Much of our today's produced wealth are actually connected with the petro (oil and gas, extraction, chemicals) industries.

Our industries and our ways of life, if we don't elect to change but progress, depends for at least for over 50% (if not more) on fossil fuels in our mix. [69]

And what should also worry us is that the Oil and Gas economies (sector, companies) around the globe are *as active as ever* in expanding, building-up so much more projects, investments, infrastructure and capacities.

Especially in Asia, Africa, Latin America and Middle-East.

Ever more.

And how do we change course in our economies and societies, if we see ourselves ever more in a competitive race for jobs, wealth, power and influence between each other?

---

[67] By actual events in our world: climate change,climate refugees, economic rivalries, crisis or volatilites,etc.
[68] California is about to find out what a truly radical climate policy looks like
[69] Never mind the risk of creative accounting and engineering in the calculus of CO2 footprint and methane emissions. If Climate Change is real- we cannot walk away from our path of duty and care.

The better "Climate Change transformational strategies" are if we recognize that we have to slow-down and transform our economies, and turn our eyes and ears towards the more holistic human and sustainable development.

Towards Laudato Si!

But how easy is this- when "the Barbarians" [70]- the others- are knocking at our gates?

Try that to explain to Rex Tillerson or Exxon Mobile. Or its' shareholders.

Or to India and China.

The failure of a reasonable and effective execution of the Paris Agreement is not so attractive.

Non-action or not enough action, will – and for starters, and let's assume for a moment that the climate science is about right- result in a rapid and irreversible detoriation in the comfort zones of our actual living conditions:

- More heat waves, storms, floods, droughts, climate victims and refugees

- More land and land places will become unattractive or dangerous to live, with ever more food crop yield at risk, or basic food scarcities.

- More unsettling of our Nature, which in itself, is already unsettled by our today's presence.

- More human emotions and sufferings between people of good will and not so good will.

- Having lost or seeing "loss of life and suffering" due to Climate Change may cause new mass refugees, terrorism, hatred, new international polarizations and new demands and calls for compensations or (international) criminal justice. [71]

The above Climate Change consequences can be "in real", or "being perceived" by people, societies and nations.

A failure in the execution of the Paris Climate Change agreement is and may be the cause of conflict, war or an ever more self-centered world ; where Parties

---

[70] Present economic, market and job rivalries between US, China, India, etc.
[71] Especially towards the US and the West. Just

are securing and grouping themselves only for their own political and national gains.

Rather Cynical and a World of Darwin. [72]

Whilst the poor and deprived in Sub-Sahara Africa and in dense-populated Asian countries are most likely to suffer from Climate Change, it are the Western Societies (US, EU, OECD) that are mostly exposed to the rise of emotions within their own societies and internationally, including the call for compensation from the rest of the world.

Political Leadership and Leadership in the Energy Sector better be warned.

It can truly become a can of worms, or a Pandora's Box.

Now – the actual signing of the Paris Climate Agreement is and has been actually the easy bit.

If we recollect how much effort it took us to get to this stage- we may rightly be a little concerned on what to expect in this next stage: its actual deliverance.

It did not ask too much from Governments, neither did it ask to commit too much.

Only a very early first stage-and only for a very limited number of years.

And we know that the aggregate of the present commitments given is far from what we need to see if we like to see ourselves out of trouble.

It's still window-dressing.

Add to that, another simple reality of today- and you may state with me:

Houston we've got a problem:

Given the speeds and acceleration of our global developments in our human development-

We actually and urgently need 17 Paris Agreements, 17 Conference of the Parties – on the attainment of the UN Sustainable Development Goals.

Today- we only have One- Or actually None![73]

---

[72] Exact the path that President Trump, Rex Tillerson and his cabinet are presently steering on, towards.
[73] With President Trump in the Whitehouse.

The Paris Climate Change Agreement.

So- you understand perhaps with me- how "Baby" we still are in the organization of our stewardship of our global village.

How "Baby" we are in managing our resources, our human development, our capabilities and capacities to change some of the directions in our industrial engineered complexes- and how remote we yet are from an adequate and performing executive organization that can zipper between the parties and partners and make things to work.

We better *converse*.

A shy call from Nature

It is no secret that Saint Francis loved the Animal Kingdom.

In fact, (and from Wikipedia) **World Animal Day** is an international day of action for animal rights and welfare celebrated annually on October 4, the feast day of Francis of Assisi, the patron saint of animals.

It started in 1931 at a convention of ecologists in Florence, Italy who wished to highlight the plight of endangered species.[

Now, Pope Francis reminded us in his Encyclical about our role, relation, position and duty of care of, over and with Creation.

Our role is to live in harmony in and with our Biodiversity and Nature.

Not in conflict. Not infringing on biodiversity and animal rights. Not killing, destroying, over-consuming or making extinct what cannot be recovered.

And stewarding the welfare of animals when under the custodianship of ourselves.

Well: *How good are we doing all this?*

Well lets' have a look at that.

From the WWF 2016 website and report on the state of our biodiversity[74], we can read:

Go to WWF Website

Quote

How many species are we losing?

Well... this is the million dollar question.

And one that's very hard to answer.

Firstly, we don't know exactly what's out there.

It's a big complex world and we discover new species to science all the time.

"Scientists were startled in 1980 by the discovery of a tremendous diversity of insects in tropical forests. In one study of just 19 trees in Panama, 80% of the 1,200 beetle species discovered were previously unknown to science... Surprisingly, scientists have a better understanding of how many stars there are in the galaxy than how many species there are on Earth." - World Resources Institute (WRI).

---

[74] Including our impacts (and over-consumption) of animals in the seas, on land, and in the skies

So, if we don't know how much there is to begin with, we don't know exactly how much we're losing.

But we do have lots of facts and figures that seem to indicate that the news isn't good.

If there are:
- **100,000,000 different species on Earth**
- **and the extinction rate is just 0.01% / year**
- *at least* **10,000 species go extinct ever year**

Just to illustrate the degree of biodiversity loss we're facing, let's take you through one scientific analysis...

- *The rapid loss of species we are seeing today is estimated by experts to be between 1,000 and 10,000 times higher than the natural extinction rate.**
- *These experts calculate that between 0.01 and 0.1% of all species will become extinct each year.*
- *If the low estimate of the number of species out there is true - i.e. that there are around 2 million different species on our planet** - then that means between 200 and 2,000 extinctions occur every year.*
- *But if the upper estimate of species numbers is true - that there are 100 million different species co-existing with us on our planet - then between 10,000 and 100,000 species are becoming extinct each year.*

Unlike the mass extinction events of geological history, the current extinction challenge is one for which a single species - ours - appears to be almost wholly responsible.

This is often referred to as the 6th extinction crisis, after the 5 known extinction waves in geological history.

So without arguing about who's right or wrong. Or what the exact numbers are.

There can be little debate that there is, in fact, a very serious biodiversity crisis.

UnQuote

I think the following press article from WWF (from 2014) states it all so much clear:

Quote

Between 1970 and 2010 populations of mammals, birds, reptiles, amphibians, and fish around the globe dropped 52 percent, says the 2014 Living Planet Report released today by World Wildlife Fund (WWF). This biodiversity loss occurs disproportionately in low-income countries—and correlates with the increasing resource use of high-income countries.

In addition to the precipitous decline in wildlife populations the report's data point to other warning signs about the overall health of the planet. The amount of carbon in our atmosphere has risen to levels not seen in more than a million years, triggering climate change that is already destabilizing ecosystems. High concentrations of reactive nitrogen are degrading lands, rivers and oceans. Stress on already scarce water supplies is increasing. And more than 60 percent of the essential "services" provided by nature, from our forests to our seas, are in decline.

"We're gradually destroying our planet's ability to support our way of life," said Carter Roberts, president and CEO of WWF. "But we already have the knowledge and tools to avoid the worst predictions. We all live on a finite planet and its time we started acting within those limits."

The Living Planet Report, WWF's biennial flagship publication, measures trends in three major areas:
• populations of more than ten thousand vertebrate species;
• human ecological footprint, a measure of consumption of goods, greenhouse gas emissions; and
• existing biocapacity, the amount of natural resources for producing food, freshwater, and sequestering carbon.

"There is a lot of data in this report and it can seem very overwhelming and complex," said Jon Hoekstra, chief scientist at WWF. "What's not complicated are the clear trends we're seeing -- 39 percent of terrestrial wildlife gone, 39 percent of marine wildlife gone, 76 percent of freshwater wildlife gone – all in the past 40 years."

The report says that the majority of high-income countries are increasingly consuming more per person than the planet can accommodate; maintaining per capita ecological footprints greater than the amount of biocapacity available per person. People in middle- and low-income countries have seen little increase in their per capita footprints over the same time period.

While high-income countries show a 10 percent increase in biodiversity, the rest of the world is seeing dramatic declines. Middle-income countries show 18 percent declines, and low-income countries show 58 percent declines. Latin

America shows the biggest decline in biodiversity, with species populations falling by 83 percent.

"High-income countries use five times the ecological resources of low-income countries, but low income countries are suffering the greatest ecosystem losses," said Keya Chatterjee, WWF's senior director of footprint. "In effect, wealthy nations are outsourcing resource depletion."

The report underscores that the declining trends are not inevitable. To achieve globally sustainable development, each country's per capita ecological footprint must be less than the per capita biocapacity available on the planet, while maintaining a decent standard of living.

At the conclusion of the report, WWF recommends the following actions:

1. Accelerate shift to smarter food and energy production
2. Reduce ecological footprint through responsible consumption at the personal, corporate and government levels
3. Value natural capital as a cornerstone of policy and development decisions

Unquote

And how do you think we are doing well with this? Also in the more developed countries around the globe?

Let me share you here a brief article from England:

England's best-loved wildlife still in serious decline, report shows

Much of England's best-loved wildlife remains in serious decline, according to the latest official assessment from the government. Birds and butterflies on farmland have continued their long term downward trend and 75% of over 200 "priority" species across the country – including hedgehogs, dormice and moths – are falling in number.

The Natural Environment Indicators for England also showed that water quality has fallen in the last five years, with just one in five rivers and lakes having high or good status, and the amount of time given by conservation volunteers has also fallen.

...

"This report paints a pretty grim picture of how our wildlife is faring in the countryside," said Sandra Bell, at Friends of the Earth. "Added to recent new evidence that wild bees have been harmed by neonicotinoid pesticides, it's clear that if we want to enjoy a thriving natural environment big changes are needed to our farming system. This must be a priority for the government as part of its Brexit strategy."

Christopher Price, at the CLA, which represents landowners, farmers and rural businesses, said: "This progress report is a tough read for all those who care about our countryside. As we prepare to exit the EU, it is clear that the new [farming and environment] policy must

have greater ambition in how it supports farmers and land managers to deliver better environmental outcomes." On Thursday, a poll showed the public strongly supports stronger post-Brexit environmental policies.

Now I come to something of importance.

First of all, I need to mention the movement and the general direction of *intensive* farming – of both animals as well as crops and soils in order to attain un-natural yields-

Intensive farming practices include growing high-yield crops, using fertilisers and pesticides and keeping animals indoors. Food production is increased but there are a gross amount of unwelcome side effects on the well-fare and well-being of animals (chickens, pigs, cows, fish, etc) , on general health (pesticides, hormones) as well long-term negative impact on soil, land and crops

Over and above this, new bio-engineering and gen-modification[75] practices of animals and crops for meat and food, has seen its' steady rise of agri-industrial interests,

In densely populated China, this practice has reached a new frontier, where moral and ethical boundaries (of humanity, animal well-fare) seem again to have been crossed.

I quote here from the Guardian NewsPapers:

A biotech consortium in China has announced that it intends to open a facility near Beijing with the aim of cloning up to a million cows a year to meet the country's growing demand for beef. The factory won't stop at cows. It also plans to clone racehorses, pets and even sniffer dogs. But the vast majority of animals it produces will be calves for meat production.

And there is also Climate Change: Climate Change is and will have its' own impact on the stability and availability of our biodiversity: our animal kingdom.

If you like to read a most concerning article on what this may do in the Pacific Ocean, I suggest you read the following news article:

The Blob That Cooked the Pacific

When a deadly patch of warm water shocked the West Coast, some feared it was a preview of our future oceans (under Climate Change)

---

[75] Monsanto

Is there any good news?

Lets' start by giving President Obama some credit: he declared words largest marine reserve offshore Hawaii – a now protected natural habitat.

World's largest marine reserve created off Hawaii

And we if look and would listen at what Scientists recommend us today to do, today, and I only speak here Oceans (and its BioDiversity) here- than the following would be a nice move:

From Pew Charitable Trust

Scientific studies often address narrowly focused questions, but sometimes scientists bundle many answers together to address bigger questions, such as how best to manage the global ocean. A just published review of previous studies, for example, contains a surprising big-picture finding: It pays to set aside at least 30 percent of the sea in marine protected areas (MPAs).

Marine reserves and other types of MPAs are widely recognized as vital for conserving both biodiversity and the fish populations needed for healthy fisheries. However, only about 2 percent of the ocean is currently set aside as fully protected MPAs. In 2010, the United Nations Convention on Biological Diversity set a target of expanding coverage to at least 10 percent of ocean waters by 2020; the full U.N. also adopted this percentage as part of its sustainable development goal on ocean conservation.

More recently, though, a consensus has been building that more might be needed. In 2014, the International Union for Conservation of Nature's World Parks Congress recommended protecting at least 30 percent.

University of York scientists Bethan O'Leary and Callum Roberts, the lead authors of the study published March 21 in the peer-reviewed journal Conservation Letters, set out to examine what targets for protection might be appropriate for different ocean management goals. They searched the scientific literature for studies that looked at a specific goal and the proportion of an ocean area that should be protected to achieve it. They found 144 studies that examined a wide range of objectives, including protecting biodiversity, ensuring that populations in different parts of a species' range can move from one MPA to another, avoiding the collapse of fisheries or specific species populations, maximizing fisheries value or yield, and minimizing trade-offs among stakeholders with at times competing interests.

The analysis in "Effective Coverage Targets for Ocean Protection" finds a remarkable consensus that protecting 30 to 40 percent of an ocean area is necessary to achieve many of these individual management goals. More than half of the 144 studies concluded that at least 30 percent of the area under consideration had to be set aside to achieve the stated goal. Only a tiny fraction found that 10 percent was sufficient.

This was true regardless of the goal being considered. In other words, if the objective is to protect biodiversity, the majority of studies suggest setting aside at least 30 percent of the management area. If it is to maximize fisheries value or yield, or to satisfy multiple stakeholders, most studies again recommend protecting at least 30 percent of those waters.

It's important to note that none of the studies looked at the global ocean in its entirety. Still, taken together, they provide solid evidence that 10 percent is not enough.

These results come at an opportune time. A U.N. Preparatory Committee looking at how to better protect international waters will start its first meeting March 28. The group will begin negotiations on an international treaty to conserve and protect marine biodiversity in areas beyond national jurisdiction, more commonly known as the high seas.

The new study provides key insights into the important role that protected areas play in achieving diverse conservation and socioeconomic goals. The findings should help advance discussions about coverage targets going forward.

Now- overlooking the above- you may ask with me.

Saint Francis- what are we to do?

Pope Francis- *how* can we get our agri-culture, our exploitation of natural resources, our dignity and respect for the Amimal Kingdom, for Nature and for all living species back into our economies, our commerce, our politics, and our societal habits and actions forwards?

Is there anything we can do to Pray and ask for Forgiveness , to reduce suffering and disseminate better insights?

Is there anything we can do than to education and rapidly diffuse our better awareness, working practices and stewardship over the Animal Kingdom around?

Is there anything we can do to protect, preserve and regulate men's actions and activities inside the natural habitats, and that need to be protected?

Is there anything we can do to grow and nurture our love for animals and to nurture our abilities to grow healthy foods at all of our children's schools and hopefully living communities around?

Is there anything we can do to learn our Leaders (in Business, in Politics, In Industries) that there is more than simply commerce, a spreadsheet, consumer needs, a yield and a margin.

Can we learn to make "Peace and All Good" between us and Animal Life?

How does this work in the different cultures, the different religions, and the different market economies around?

Have we really done all and every efforts *in the forms and formats* of our organizations (cross the Globe) to see this right?

Well- you may appreciate from me- I cannot answer all of the above questions.

But what I *do* know is that again Pope Francis saw right.

This is the moment.

These are the years- that we individually and collectively- determine what will be about of our nature, of our bio-diversity, and of the integrity and well-being of the original species of Planet Earth.

This is the moment that we may need to see ourselves in the mirror, and make-up our minds: Does the "above signs and signals" on the well-being of the Animal Kingdom and Nature reflects anything of the *actual* well-being of ourselves?

No better moment to convene in Assisi, and to share and discuss how we can improve "*our Peace between Ourselves and Nature* (Animal Kingdom)" and our ways of communication, education and organization- such that we can *truly* steward Nature and see this change challenge about.

Good Governance, Freedom and Peace

I like this age and time. I was born lucky.

I was born in the early 60's – and my life has been blessed with a good upbringing, joyful and happy times in my youth, excellent education, friends and family and career opportunities in an international professional life and work setting, second to none, - and almost as in a dream.

My life has also brought me on the path of self-realisation and some time for a deeper nurturing of my self-awareness and consciousness- "off the beaten path" - so to speak- and that has made me into the man I presently am.

I was born in North-West Europe, grew partially up in the Caribbean, and have seen and travelled quite some of our world.

What I do *see* is that it takes courage and self-leadership to live free, and it takes leadership[76] and maturity to serve and nurture a social community, company or nation to allow the members live as free as realistically can be.[77]

What I also see is a remarkable journey in time, and with the last century of truly astonishing human development with all its' progress and forms, not in the least by all of the scientific, technology, innovations and businesses.

We all know and we all may be aware of the differences in States, Governments and Constitutions- in the East (e.g. China) and the West (e.g. USA).

> - Different concepts.
>
> - Different cultural and historic backgrounds.
>
> - Different forms and performances
>
> - Different national and individual ambition levels
>
> - Different understanding of what Free and Freedom means and implies.

One thing we all may agree on:

Freedom, responsibility, joy and care are not each others' enemy.

In fact- they go hand-in hand.

---

[76] Stewardship for the next generation

[77] In our present Catholic Church leadership- some very good examples of how this can be done has been demonstrated by Pope John Paul II and now Pope Francis

If I use the earlier words spoken by Pope Francis- you may recognize with me, what I do here imply and mean:

As proposed in Evangelii Gaudium: "sobriety, when lived freely and consciously, is liberating" (223), just as "happiness means knowing how to limit some needs which only diminish us, and being open to the many different possibilities which life can offer" (223). In this way "we must regain the conviction that we need one another, that we have a shared responsibility for others and the world, and that being good and decent are worth it" (229).

The saints accompany us on this journey. Saint Francis, cited several times, is "the example par excellence of care for the vulnerable and of an integral ecology lived out joyfully and authentically" (10). He is the model of "the inseparable bond between concern for nature, justice for the poor, commitment to society, and interior peace" (10). The Encyclical also mentions Saint Benedict, Saint Teresa di Lisieux and Blessed Charles de Foucauld.

We also know of that with the rise of average mean wealth and income, the people in a Nation (and very generally speaking) can become more self-reliant and self-aware: seeking, asking or demanding more freedoms[78] - in work and life- and expressing themselves with ever more freedoms.

The countries in Scandinavia are often used as a better example- and case in time.[79]

But we also know, and may have experienced or seen, that (un-guided) freedom can or may lead to excessive, erratic and/or unconstrained behaviours.

Freedoms without responsibility and a connectedness to a purposeful meaning in community- can corrupt or may lead people astray, and away from their healthier selves.

We have seen and witnessed this in our corporate and financial sectors of our societies.[80]

We have seen and witnessed this in the up-rise of violence or number of imprisonments for drug dealings or abuse- in e.g. the American prison system.

And we see this in the at present populist and xenophobic times, (greed, fear, self-interests[81]) reactions in some of the West., putting the dream of a truly free society in and between people from different race, religion, ethnicity ever so much away.

---

[78] From a central state and/or corporation,

[79] Having worked and lives in North-West Europe and Scandinavia – I can assure you that even here we have much learnings to do. It is clearly still a work in progress.

[80] Financial Crisis, Banking Scandals, Panama Files, Volkswagen, BP, Wolf of Wall Street.

[81] America First and populist movementin Europe

Fear for freedom- Every Human Being Counts

Governments in countries have been historically tasked to manage and lead the Commons: the public space- in and between the People of a Nation.

Laws, regulations and supervisory (governance) controls are, very generally speaking, the appointed instruments- in order to do so.

To rule by (Common) Law.

To rule by Good Governance

Fear for "chaos and dis-order" in the Public Domain, through the more un-disciplined and un-guided forms of people's expressions, rivalling or self-interests- is, at times, and to some degree- the source and inspiration of state laws, regulations and supervisory controls.

To maintain control

To upkeep order

To focus on the Commons, National and International interests

The present perceived erosion and weakening of (some) government controls and national performances[82] in the "so-called" populist or more "free national democracies" of the West[83], may be the source of inspiration *and* justification to some leading authoritarian states and state leaderships to proceed with the present elected centralized and more strong governance model, and ways of maintaining order and control over the nation and population.[84][85]

The rivalry and competition between the Eastern Governance Model (e.g. China, Russia) and Western Governance model (e.g. USA) surely another factor "shaping and pulling" at the social fabric of many countries and governments abound.

---

[82] Polarizations and indeciveness in politics and societies. Weak EU and Crazy (angry) USA, where democrats and Republicans show as no other how democracies can be seen to fail.
[83] "Weak West"
[84] President Putin and Xi are often quoted here.
[85] 2016 Freedom House Report: https://freedomhouse.org/sites/default/files/FH_FITW_Report_2016.pdf

On this, the 2016 Freedom House report made the following more sober observations.

And I quote :

> *The world was battered by crises that fueled xenophobic sentiment in democratic countries, undermined the economies of states dependent on the sale of natural resources, and led authoritarian regimes to crack down harder on dissent. These developments contributed to the 10th consecutive year of decline in global freedom.*
>
> - *The number of countries showing a decline in freedom for the year—72—was the largest since the 10-year slide began. Just 43 countries made gains.*
>
> - *Over the past 10 years, 105 countries have seen a net decline, and only 61 have experienced a net improvement.*
>
> - *Ratings for the Middle East and North Africa region were the worst in the world in 2015, followed closely by Eurasia.*
>
> - *Over the last decade, the most significant global reversals have been in freedom of expression and the rule of law.*

But let's proceed a little with our discussion and exploration.

Let's agree- that our Nations are truly diverse in culture, development stages and historic backgrounds, and that in some countries and cultures, the State or the Commons are seen as more important than the private individual.

So in essence:

Different Countries. Different Stages of Development. Different Maturities. Different Operating Models.[86]

Add to this a fact, and that we know first-hand from our own history, is that when people are feeling oppressed and dominated by a single elite or doctrine, that the people become either lethargic in their commitments, out of fear, or –

and if the surpression of the (individual) freedoms and thoughts are pressed *too far*- ultimately erupts in a fierce from of resistance and fight for freedom.[87][88]

---

[86] But with people, animals and nature living in them

[87] Flight, fight or freeze

[88] Poland under Second World War and thereafter: Nazi and Russian Occupations.

People – when not feeling *free*[89] enough, combined with unjust rulings from an elite (power inequality) in a Nation (or Corporations)- may seek to stand-up, call and organize for action and change.[90]

This was true in the times of the Bastille. This was true for America's Independence and this may become true for a range of Nations today.

In the East and in the West. The North and the South.

It's a "fine balancing and art" of true (inspired) statesmanship to bring a people and nation into development *and* freedom.

The rise and fall of "the Arab Spring" – and it's chaos- can be seen as a most recent example and almost *lost case* in time.

I have lived and worked in Damascus, Syria. In the mid 90's.

I have first-hand experienced the order and relative calm and prosperity of the Nation, under its' regime of a self-elected, and elite leadership.

I have first-hand seen and experienced what the cult of a National police, security and intelligence services can do in the social fabric of a Nation : it affects the mutual trusts and feelings of compassion and freedom between the people in a Nation.[91]

Lack of (human dignity and social) freedoms – over some amount of time-results in conflict.

It's as simple as this.

And we have now all seen and witnessed first-hand what a new game of geo-politics by the Super-Powers can do inside an unbalanced society.

How many more Syria's[92] will our world have, before we come to understand that it all starts at the very micro-level and basis of our communities and care:

How free and tolerant in mind are we and how much freedom can we allow and share with the other?

---

[89] In mind, words or movements: political, religious, social, intellectual, etc.

[90] Private Wealth and Royal Families (in e.g. Europe) and Owners of Large Corporations know this fact as well, as no other

[91] Or so you wish, and in the most horrific examples- please refer to Pope John Paul Ii stories on Nazi Germany and Russia's Stalin occupation of Poland.

[92] Syrian Civil War is and has been aggrevated by the Supoer-Powers at Play in and over Syria. This form of geo-politics and civil war-game between rivalling blocks (Russa, US, Iran/China) is a very concerning situation for our world at large.

How responsible and caring are we towards the other- and who is of a different origin?[93]

Have we managed to become true stewards of responsible, joyful and caring freedom?

Have we learned to become members of a Free Society- to live freely, caring, responsibly and together?

Living together in one nation, with many different races, ethnicities, religious and political / private wealth elite can be complicated.

Can be rather Fear-some.

Just think for a moment of what it takes to govern India or lead China.

Two point four (2.4) billion people are presently living in and under these two proud nations.

Our world and global health has *never ever* been so dependent on the health, freedom and peace of the human development and social behaviours in and fo these countries, as well in the patters of behaviours they extend into their spheres of national and economic (military) interest and in relation (or rivalry) to the developed nations of the OECD.

May we seek forgiveness of our past mistakes, and may we seek guidance for our *shared* leadership and pathways forwards:

Helping our people to become true free citizens of free nations abound.

May we hope that, "Good Governance" and " (Individual) Freedom" or – "Human Dignity" - have become, as such, two sides of the same coin.

"Good Governance, Freedom and Peace" are and have become "a New Trinity" – nationally and internationally- in our aspirations to attain the Paris Climate Agreement and the UN Sustainable Development Goals.

Without them- our endeavours will be hopeless and in vain.

So- in order to attain Sustainable Development- our eyes and ears cannot be moved away from the issue of "Good Governance, Freedom and Peace" .

They are inter-related.

May you live and work "in Freedom and in Peace".

May you see Good Governance.

---

[93] President's Xi Jipping most recent 1st july address on the 95th anniversary of the CPC tells some , and that may concerns us today.

Chapter 2: Conversions

Small Tales of Religious Conversion

If we like to come to speak about modern day *change and transformation, or better* - *conversion* - of ourselves and societies , then we cannot ignore the human condition and societal developments and conversions that have taken place in the past.

It is by our willingness and our readiness to stand on the shoulders of those who have led us to the place of where we are today- that we can learn and see to become our better selves- and see where our humanity, today, invites us to go.

Let me take you on a small journey of some typical conversions that have taken place in our world, and that *we – all around the world-* may have want to know, hear of or would benefit from if we make time and wanting to understand.

My intent is not to be exhaustive or complete, but just to touch upon some typical world changing conversions that have taken place over our period of history and time.

In this section of small tales of conversion, I like to touch base with some examples of spiritual/religious- , conversions and events that has helped to shape our world.

These conversions have shaped us. They have made us into the world and civilization that we are today.

Some of these conversions have taken time and were quite evolutionary, others appeared in revolution.

 Some conversions were initiated by groups of people and turned into a movement of change.

Other conversions were inspired and initiated by a single human being- even a single event- and that has helped to change the minds and lives of people- all around the world.

Some were helpful in changing the course and direction of our human civilisation and were only active or remembered over a short period of time.

Others have become known because of their long-lasting and much longer wave impact and influence in and over our civilisation and lives.

But let me begin.

Let me start with the spiritual/ religious dimensions of our present world and world order.

It was Jesus of Nazareth, "the Son of God" to Christians who are in faith, that brought an impulse and conversion into our world order, second to none, and that has crossed time and space- and is still very much alive, relevant and active today.

For some, Jesus' gift was not only his passion, crucifiction, re-demption of sins, and re-surrection, but is and has also been and seen in his life, wisdom and stories, prophecies, miracles, attention for the poor and needy and the healing of men.-

For some- Jesus' gift was expressed by his compassionate love for every human being ("love thy neighbor as thyself") ,- his Sermon on the Mount- as well his message of direct communion with the Divine ("Our Holy Father" - prayer).

In any shape or form, Jesus stood on the shoulders of those that has led him before, and took new and fresh eyes on the religious experience.

It was Jesus' who shook the (religious leadership and) establishment awake, and that led people to reflect on the logic and rules applied when speaking with or over God or relate between themselves in community, in religion and in communion.[94]

It has been the combination of those (life-changing) impulses that has made Jesus- in what he still very much is today.

Now you don't need to be a religious expert or man or woman of faith, to know and understand with me that the organizational form of Christianity, and over the years, has taken many different shapes and forms.

Men and women, and over time, has given his own interpretation on the exactitude of Jesus teachings, meanings and intents.

Men and women, and over time, have mended Christianity or the Church in order to better serve self, worldly leadership (state) needs or (state) interests, as such preventing the world from achieving the ideals Jesus pro-claimed, now some 2000 years ago.

Despite further a history of inquisition, crusades, wars, conflicts of interests, reformations, fragmentations and human tragedies and scandals- The Church and with all its' (long-wave) resonance, impulse and teachings of Loving Kindness and Compassion[95]- is today still very much alive and sparkling, and is with over 2 billion baptized Christians *all over the planet*, celebrating this largest religion alive.

The positive inspiration and life-giving impulse of Jesus cannot be denied nor understated.

The attraction and compassion of the present religious leadership of the Church embodied in Pope Francis can simply not be ignored or denied.

---

[94] For secular or different religious people- it may be instrumental to watch some of the words of Cardinal Pietro Parolin at WEF Davos 2017

[95] Christ-Love or simple Human Dignity: Cardinal Pietro Parolin at WEF Davos 2017

But let me be clear here.

That same sense of miracle and wonder can be found in the other world religions, be it in the life and words of the Buddha, Muhammed or the Bhaghawan Gita (Hindu), Confucius/Tao.

And the same stories of conversions can be seen and learned.

It was the Siddhartha Gautama, the rich prince from Lumbini, the house of Suddhodana, an elected chief of the Shakya clan, that needed to escape and go out of his secluded and safe zone created by his Father in order to see and experience with his own eyes what poverty and human suffering around him was, and to learn - with his own body and mind- what this suffering is and what it means and does to the "human gestalt" .

Through his search of extreme forms of suffering, fasting and meditation– in body and in mind- the Buddha was able to receive and find the intensity of Peace, Calm, Detachment and Enlightenment.

"A State of Being" he kept for the rest of his life, and allowed him to share and gift his community of followers and fellows an example of mastery and wisdom, including his jewels and views on the four noble truth and the eightfold path rules for a good life - seldomly seen or heard before.

From Wikipedia

In time, "liberating insight" became an essential feature of the Buddhist tradition. The following teachings, which are commonly seen as essential to Buddhism, are later formulations which form part of the explanatory framework of this "liberating insight":[121][120]

- The Four Noble Truths: that suffering is an ingrained part of existence; that the origin of suffering is craving for sensuality, acquisition of identity, and fear of annihilation; that suffering can be ended; and that following the Noble Eightfold Path is the means to accomplish this;
- The Noble Eightfold Path: right view, right intention, right speech, right action, right livelihood, right effort, right mindfulness, and right concentration;
- Dependent origination: the mind creates suffering as a natural product of a complex process.

The eight Buddhist concepts in the Noble Eightfold Path are,

(from Wikipedia)

1. *right view: the belief that there is an afterlife, that not everything ends with death, that Buddha taught and followed a successful path to nirvana;[25][27][28] According to Peter Harvey, the first concept in the path is to inculcate a belief in the Buddhist principles of karma and rebirth, and the importance of the Four Noble Truths and the True Realities.[29]*
2. *right resolve: the giving up home and adopting the life of a religious mendicant in order to follow the path; this concept, states Harvey, aims at peaceful renunciation, into an environment of non-sensuality, non-ill-will (to lovingkindness), away from cruelty (to compassion).[30] Such an environment aids contemplation of impermanence, suffering, and non-Self.[30]*
3. *right speech: no lying, no rude speech, no telling one person what another says about him, speaking that which leads to salvation;*
4. *right conduct: no killing or injuring, no taking what is not given, no sexual acts.*
5. *right livelihood: beg to feed, only possessing what is essential to sustain life;*
6. *right effort: guard against sensual thoughts; this concept, states Harvey, aims at preventing unwholesome states that disrupt meditation.[30]*
7. *right mindfulness: never be absent minded, conscious of what one is doing; this, states Harvey, encourages the mindfulness about impermanence of body, feeling and mind, as well as to experience the five skandhas, the five hindrances, the four True Realities and seven factors of awakening.[30]*
8. *right samadhi (concentration): practicing four stages of dhyana meditation.*

The Buddha has become the example to many of how to live a better life, in the ever more complex and demanding modern times.

People feel inspired to create a (more detached) Zen Buddhism feeling of quiet, calm and serenity – in their homes as well in offices alike.

It is this more deeper felt peace, tranquillity, non-separation and good intent that may be of help to us to build bridges of understanding between ourselves, and to make the room and place for more peace in our busi-ness-

Muhammed- The holy Prophet and Founder of Islam

(from Wikipedia)

Born approximately 570 CE in the Arabian city of Mecca, Muhammad was orphaned at an early age; he was raised under the care of his paternal uncle Abu Talib. Periodically, he would retreat to a cave named Hira in the mountains for several nights of seclusion and prayer; later, at age 40, he reported being visited by Gabriel in the cave,[8][9][10][11] where he stated he received his first revelation from God. Three years later Muhammad started preaching these revelations publicly,[12] proclaiming that "God is One", that complete "surrender" (lit. _islām_) to him is the only way (_dīn_)[n 3] acceptable to God, and that he was a prophet and messenger of God, similar to the other prophets in Islam.[13][14][15]

Muhammad gained few early followers, and met hostility from some Meccan tribes. To escape persecution, Muhammad sent some followers to Abyssinia before he and his followers migrated from Mecca to Medina (then known as Yathrib) in the year 622. This event, the Hijra, marks the beginning of the Islamic calendar, also known as the Hijri Calendar. In Medina, Muhammad united the tribes under the Constitution of Medina. In December 629, after eight years of intermittent conflict with Meccan tribes, Muhammad gathered an army of 10,000 Muslim converts and marched on the city of Mecca. The attack went largely uncontested and Muhammad seized the city with little bloodshed. He destroyed 360 pagan idols at the Kaaba.[16] In 632, a few months after returning from the Farewell Pilgrimage, Muhammad fell ill and died. Before his death, most of the Arabian Peninsula had converted to Islam.[17][18]

The revelations (each known as _Ayah_, lit. "Sign [of God]"), which Muhammad reported receiving until his death, form the verses of the Quran, regarded by Muslims as the "Word of God" and around which the religion is based. Besides the Quran, Muhammad's teachings and practices (_sunnah_), found in the Hadith and _sira_ literature, are also upheld by Muslims and used as sources of Islamic law (see Sharia).

The first sura of the Quran is repeated in the five daily prayers and in other occasions. This sura, which consists of seven verses, is the most often recited sura of the Quran:[1]

Praised be God, Lord of the Universe, the Beneficent, the Merciful and Master of the Day of Judgment, You alone We do worship and from You alone we do seek assistance, guide us to the right path, the path of those to whom You have granted blessings, those who are neither subject to Your anger nor have gone astray."[64]

Arabic	English

الله أكبر الله اكبر

God is greatest! God is greatest!

الله أكبر فوق كيد المعتدي
الله للمظلوم خير مؤيدي
أنا باليقين وبالسلاح سأفتدي
بلدي ونور الحق يسطع في يدي
قولوا معي قولوا معي
الله الله الله أكبر

God is greatest! God is greatest!
And God is greatest above plots of the aggressors,
And God is the best helper of the oppressed.
With faith and with weapons I shall defend my country
And the light of truth will shine in my hand.
Say with me! Say with me!
God, God, God is greatest!
God is above any attacker

الله فوق المعتدي

يا هذه الدنيا أطلي واسمعي

Oh this world, watch and listen:

جيش الأعادي جاء يبغي مصرعي
بالحق سوف أرده وبمدفعي
وإذا فنيت فسوف أفنيه معي
قولوا معي قولوا معي
الله الله الله اكبر

The enemy came coveting my position,
I shall fight with Truth and defenses
And if I die, I'll take him with me!
Say it with me, say it with me:
God, God, God is greatest!
God is above any attacker!

الله فوق المعتدي

الله أكبر الله أكبر

قولوا معي الويل للمستعمر
والله فوق الغادر المتجبر
الله أكبر يا بلادي كبري
وخذي بناصية المغير ودمري
قولوا معي قولوا معي
الله الله الله أكبر

God is greatest! God is greatest!
Say With Me Woe To The Colonialist
And God is Over The Invader Egotist,
God Greatest My Country Say with Me:
And Behold of Enemies Forelock and Destroy it
Say it with me, say it with me:
God, God, God is the Greatest
God is above any attacker!

الله فوق المعتدي

(source Wikipedia: Allah Akhbar- hymn song , and used as National Anthem of Lybian (until 2011) and also used during Egyptian Suez war in 1956. Song still song over the present Middle-East)

(From WikiPedia)

Hinduism is a major world religion, or a way of life,[note 1] originated from Indian subcontinent and found most notably in India and Nepal. It influenced the cultures and life styles of many Asian and South East Asian countries. With over one billion followers,[web 1] Hinduism is the world's third largest religion by population, and the majority religion in India, Nepal, Mauritius and Bali (Indonesia). Hinduism has been called the "oldest religion" in the world,[note 2] with some practitioners and scholars refer to it as *Sanātana Dharma*, "the eternal law" or the "eternal way"[4] beyond human origins.[5] Scholars regard Hinduism as a fusion[note 3] or synthesis[6][note 4] of various Indian cultures and traditions,[7][note 5] with diverse roots[8][note 6] and no founder.[9] This "Hindu synthesis" started to develop between 500 BCE and 300 CE,[10] after the Vedic times.[10][11]

Although Hinduism contains a broad range of philosophies, it is linked by shared concepts, recognisable rituals, cosmology, shared textual resources, pilgrimage to sacred sites and the questioning of authority.[12] Hindu texts are classified into Shruti ("heard") and Smriti ("remembered"). These texts discuss theology, philosophy, mythology, Vedic yajna, Yoga and agamic rituals and temple building, among other topics.[13] Major scriptures include the Vedas and Upanishads, the Bhagavad Gita, and the Agamas.[14][15]

Prominent themes in Hindu beliefs include the four *Puruṣārthas*, the proper goals or aims of human life, namely Dharma (ethics/duties), Artha (prosperity/work), Kama (desires/passions) and Moksha (liberation/freedom);[16][17] *karma* (action, intent and consequences), *samsara* (cycle of rebirth), and the various Yogas (paths or practices to attain moksha).[18][19] Hindu practices include rituals such as puja (worship) and recitations, meditation, family-oriented rites of passage, annual festivals, and occasional pilgrimages. Some Hindus leave their social world and material possessions, then engage in lifelong Sannyasa (monastic practices) to achieve moksha.[20][21] Hinduism prescribes the eternal duties, such as honesty, refraining from injuring living beings (ahimsa), patience, forbearance, self-restraint, and compassion, among others.[w]

From a single Religion into Interfaith religion and Global Peace-building: The Spirit of Assisi.

But we live in a time and age whereby *all* people , and *all* countries of the world, and thanks to the gift of mobility, communication and transportation have become ever more connected and inter-connected.

It has been the recognition of this phenomena, including the insight and inspiration that (spirituality &) faith is not hold to one religion, one race, one country, one truth or one people- that the Catholic Church, and in its' second Vatican Council allowed for opening-up and outreach to *all* religions, and *all* people of this world[96].

It was in Assisi, and in 1986, that Pope John Paul II organized a *first-ever* world conference and prayer day between *all* the religions of this world.

A breakthrough event and day - not seen or experienced *ever* before- and that gave birth to the words and meaning " The Spirit of Assisi".

An event that has continued – and now for over 30 years- till today.[97]

Knowing some of the life and works of Saint Pope John Paul II may help you to understand the magnitude and enormity of this event and setting.

Pope John Paul II, was born as Karol Jozef Wojtyla in the Polish town Wadowice, in 1920, just before the Second World War.

It was and has been the Second World War that may have helped to shape and form the life and later legacy of this- by Catholics beloved Saint John Paul the Great.

His call to Priest and Ordination came into the times of the war, and during the extreme suppressions and sufferings put on and over the Polish People by the German Nazi regime.

His first-hand witnessing of many unimaginable extremes, violences, hatred, suppressions, despairs, killings and mass death sentences of the Jews, and put on the Polish People by the German occupation,

...in combination with the sheer arrogance, ignorance, nihilsm and darkness in the Nazi Leadership - created the conditions and inspiration in this young Priest of an ever more and deeper rooted conviction and Faith.

Evermore moving into the Light. Evermore moving into a deeper compassion for Humanity.

Evermore becoming a true instrument for Peace and God's hand.

(from Wikipedia- to be used and inserted----)

---

[96] Some early pioneering work to that extend was done by Father Maximillian Mizzi, OFM Conv. in Assisi

[97] The Spirit Of Assisi: http://lospiritodiassisi.org/cefid_eng.html

He was one of the most travelled world leaders in history, visiting 129 countries during his pontificate.. His wish was "to place his Church at the heart of a new religious alliance that would bring together Jews, Muslims and Christians in a great religious armada".

Now you may perhaps better understand with me- why Assisi, and why this conversion led by Pope John Paul II into our times, is such of significance and importance.

Let me try to explain:

When you have seen in the abyss of humanity, when you have first-handed witnessed the awful truth of the shadow sides and abilities of our humanity- that men and women are able to ruthlessly dominate, kill and suppress other living human beings- and go to war- you change.

You change either for the worse, becoming cynical, addicted and entangled in this web of power, violence, domination and hatred,

...or you *converse* into an "Enlighted State of Being"- a conscious leader:

You see and recognise that we are *all* part and member of one human family, and that our better acts and goals in life are achieved when we reach out- and recognize the other as brothers and sisters of ourselves.

That we allow, nourish, tolerate and enjoy the richness and diversity of *every* human being and *every* living creature on our Planet Earth.

That we become a "Lighthouse" and a messenger of that what we hold true:

Peace on Earth and (only!) All Good.

That our inner wish and drive becomes an ever deeper commitment to create this holding space and conditions- in and between ourselves- for a good and peaceful life (to all).

Conversion.

That is the significance of Pope John Paul II's message, life and organization of the interfaith dialogue events:

This is the message of a man who has been in Deep care for our Humanity and in Communion with God:

Let us please choose to be and become our better selves- crossing borders, crossing silo's and crossing working interests.[98]

Let me conclude with one other small observation:

Our present day geo-politics of emotions, acceleration of economies, the head-lines in our newspapers and social media on terror, conflicts or wars, and the , at times, rivalries and competitions between nations, leaders and in corporations- in

---

[98] Cardinal Pietro Parolin at WEF Davos 2017

rat-race and so on, does not necessarily breath or create the conditions for this better form of Peace.

The UN Sustainable development agenda includes the wish and goals for Peace and Social Justice.

It is my more humble observation that we may want *to learn* from 'the Spirit of Assisi' , and bring this "state of being" ever so much more into our world and leadership of our Corporates , Businesses, International UN Development Agencies, International Relationships and in our Governance of Cities, Societies and Nations, around our world.

The need for "the Spirit of Assisi" has *never ever* been so great in our world, as today.[99]

27 October 1986- The start of the Spirit of Assisi[100]-

At present, a small organisation[101], staffed by Friars from the Saint Francis' Friars Minor Conventual Order is leading and progressing this inter-religious peace-building initiative.

[99] Cardinal Pietro Parolin at WEF Davos 2017
[100] Day captured in Book : Assisi Profezia di Pace
[101] The CEFID – international Franciscan Centre for Dialogue http://lospiritodiassisi.org

Pope Francis and Laudato Si!

Let me move now to more contemporary religious leadership alive.

And let me move to the words and guidance of Pope Francis and his Encylical Laudato Si!

Well first of all, let us look at what type of man Pope Francis is.

From Wikipedia-

Pope Francis (Latin: *Franciscus*; Italian: *Francesco*; Spanish: *Francisco*; born **Jorge Mario Bergoglio**,[b] 17 December 1936) is the 266th and current Pope of the Roman Catholic Church, a title he holds *ex officio* as Bishop of Rome, and Sovereign of the Vatican City. He chose Francis as his papal name in honor of Saint Francis of Assisi. Francis is the first Jesuit pope, the first from the Americas, the first from the Southern Hemisphere and the first non-European pope since the Syrian Gregory III, who died in 741.

Born in Buenos Aires, Argentina, Bergoglio worked briefly as a chemical technologist and nightclub bouncer[2] before beginning seminary studies. He was ordained a Catholic priest in 1969, and from 1973 to 1979 was Argentina's provincial superior of the Society of Jesus. He was accused of handing two priests to the National Reorganization Process during the Dirty War, but the lawsuit was ultimately dismissed. He became the Archbishop of Buenos Aires in 1998, and was created a cardinal in 2001 by Pope John Paul II. He led the Argentine Church during the December 2001 riots in Argentina, and the administrations of Néstor Kirchner and Cristina Fernández de Kirchner considered him a political rival. Following the resignation of Pope Benedict XVI on 28 February 2013, a papal conclave elected Bergoglio as his successor on 13 March.

Throughout his public life, Pope Francis has been noted for his humility, emphasis on God's mercy, concern for the poor, and commitment to interfaith dialogue. He is credited with having a humble, less formal approach to the papacy than his predecessors, for instance choosing to reside in the *Domus Sanctae Marthae* guesthouse rather than in the papal apartments of the Apostolic Palace used by his predecessors. In addition, due to of ornamentation, including refusing the traditional papal mozzetta cape upon his election, choosing silver instead of gold for his piscatory ring, and keeping the same pectoral cross he had as Cardinal. He maintains that the church should be more open and welcoming. He does not support unbridled capitalism, Marxism, or Marxist versions of liberation theology. Francis maintains the traditional views of the church regarding abortion, euthanasia, contraception, homosexuality, ordination of women, and priestly celibacy. He opposes consumerism, irresponsible development, and supports taking action on climate change, a focus of his papacy with the promulgation of *Laudato si'*. In international diplomacy, he helped to restore full diplomatic relations between the U.S. and Cuba.

Lord, make me an instrument of your peace,
Where there is hatred, let me sow love;
where there is injury, pardon;
where there is doubt, faith;
where there is despair, hope;
where there is darkness, light;
where there is sadness, joy;

O Divine Master, grant that I may not so much seek to be consoled as to
console;
to be understood as to understand;
to be loved as to love.

For it is in giving that we receive;

With his Encyclical Laudato Si!, Pope Francis truly expresses who he is, and what eyes he has bestowed upon us- and invites us to *see* and *be* with him:

Using some the words from Laudato Si! may explain this the best.

(From Laudato Si!)

"What kind of world do we want to leave to those who come after us, to children who are now growing up?" (160). This question is at the heart of Laudato si' (May You be praised), the Encyclical on the care of the common home by Pope Francis.

"This question does not have to do with the environment alone and in isolation; the issue cannot be approached piecemeal".

This leads us to ask ourselves about the meaning of existence and its values at the basis of social life: "What is the purpose of our life in this world? What is the goal of our work and all our efforts?

What need does the earth have of us?" "Unless we struggle with these deeper issues – says the Pope– I do not believe that our concern for ecology will produce significant results" (160).

===

Several main themes run through the text that are addressed from a variety of different perspectives, traversing and unifying the text:

*the intimate relationship between the poor and the fragility of the planet,

*the conviction that everything in the world is connected,

*the critique of new paradigms and forms of power derived from technology,

*the call to seek other ways of understanding the economy and progress,

*the value proper to each creature,

*the human meaning of ecology,

*the need for forthright and honest debate,

*the serious responsibility of international and local policies,

(end of quote)

Best to read Laudato Si! yourself - and visit one of the better websites by the Vatican or the Catholic Community. [102]

In Appendix 1: Laudato Si! – A Map- you can find an easy to digest summary of the main highlights and essential points of the key Encyclical from our beloved Pope Francis.

---

[102] http://catholicclimatemovement.global/laudatosi/
https://laudatosi.com/watch

Jubilee Year of Mercy (2015-2016)

Now- as if all things come together in one year, Year 2015-2016 has also be declared a Jubilee Year of Mercy.

Of opening "the doors of the Church" to enter, and to ask for Mercy, for Forgiveness (for past mistakes).

Jubilee means a moment of happiness. It is par excellence a year of reconciliation, **conversion** and of sacramental penance. It takes it name from the Hebrew word for Jubilee, i.e. the word Jobel (meaning goat, referring to the ram's horn blown in religious ceremonies). The Jubilee year is especially the year of Christ.

In the words of Pope Francis:

I have decided to announce an Extraordinary Jubilee which has its centre the mercy of God. It will be a Holy Year of Mercy. We want to live in the light of the word of the Lord: "be merciful, even as your Father is merciful"

Now – during the year- Pope Francis made several gestures of what this mercifulness and forgiveness can mean- in and between ourselves.

The washing of the feet at Easter Weekend and of some (Syrian) Refugees- has not be the least of the symbolic acts of mercy, and kindness (compassion, caring) – that this (wonderful) religious moral leader has shown us over the year.

But Pope Francis shared also some special lectures and speeches on this issue.

Also here in Assisi

Meditation by His Holiness Pope Francis

Basilica of Saint Mary of the Angels, Porziuncola - Assisi
Thursday, 4 August 2016

The problem, unfortunately, comes whenever we have to deal with a brother or sister who has even slightly offended us. The reaction described in the parable describes it perfectly: "He seized him by the throat and said, 'Pay what you owe!'" (*Mt* 18:28). Here we encounter all the drama of our human relationships. When we are indebted to others, we expect mercy; but others are indebted to us, we demand justice! All of us do this. It is a reaction unworthy of Christ's disciples, nor is it the sign of a Christian style of life. Jesus teaches us to forgive and to do so limitlessly: "I do not say to you seven times, but seventy times seven" (v. 22). What he offers us is the Father's love, not our own claims to justice. To trust in the latter alone would not be the sign that we are Christ's disciples, who have obtained mercy at the foot of the cross solely by virtue of the love of the Son of God. Let us not forget, then, the harsh saying at the end of the parable: "So also my heavenly Father will do to every one of you, if you do not forgive your brother from your heart" (v. 35).

In this Holy Year of Mercy, it becomes ever clearer that the path of forgiveness can truly renew the Church and the world. To offer today's world the witness of mercy is a task from which none of us can feel exempted. I repeat: to offer today's world the witness of mercy is a task from which none of us can feel exempted. The world needs forgiveness; too many people are caught up in resentment and harbour hatred, because they are incapable of forgiving. They ruin their own lives and the lives of those around them rather than finding the joy of serenity and peace. Let us ask Saint Francis to intercede for us, so that we may always be humble signs of forgiveness and channels of mercy.

...

In my own simple words:

Forgiveness is our path to Mercy and Reconciliation-.

To Human Dignity.

Forgiveness of the other, and seeking forgiveness for ourselves, for past mistakes- is our entrance and door towards "Peace and All Good".

So- if we care to progress and positively build, stone-by-stone, brick-by-brick our world into a better place (Paris Climate Change Agreement, UN Sustainable Development), we cannot progress properly if we do not know how to forgive, and seek forgiveness of our own mistakes.

We cannot build a better world, if we do not know-how to include the others in this plan.

It's that simple.

Let me share you now also some key speeches and moral thoughts from Pope Francis over the year 2015-2016- and to our world leaders.

Meeting with the members of the General Assembly of the United Nations organization

ADDRESS OF THE HOLY FATHER

United Nations Headquarters, New York
Friday, 25 September 2015

[Multimedia]

Mr President,
Ladies and Gentlemen,

Good day. Once again, following a tradition by which I feel honored, the Secretary General of the United Nations has invited the Pope to address this distinguished assembly of nations. In my own name, and that of the entire Catholic community, I wish to express to you, Mr Ban Ki-moon, my heartfelt gratitude. I greet the Heads of State and Heads of Government present, as well as the ambassadors, diplomats and political and technical officials accompanying them, the personnel of the United Nations engaged in this 70th Session of the General Assembly, the personnel of the various programs and agencies of the United Nations family, and all those who, in one way or another, take part in this meeting. Through you, I also greet the citizens of all the nations represented in this hall. I thank you, each and all, for your efforts in the service of mankind.

This is the fifth time that a Pope has visited the United Nations. I follow in the footsteps of my predecessors Paul VI, in1965, John Paul II, in 1979 and 1995, and my most recent predecessor, now Pope Emeritus Benedict XVI, in 2008. All of them expressed their great esteem for the Organization, which they considered the appropriate juridical and political response to this present moment of history, marked by our technical ability to overcome distances and frontiers and, apparently, to overcome all natural limits to the exercise of power. An essential response, inasmuch as technological power, in the hands of nationalistic or falsely universalist ideologies, is capable of perpetrating tremendous atrocities. I can only reiterate the appreciation expressed by my predecessors, in reaffirming the importance which the Catholic Church attaches to this Institution and the hope which she places in its activities.

The United Nations is presently celebrating its seventieth anniversary. The history of this organized community of states is one of important common achievements over a period of unusually fast-paced changes. Without claiming to be exhaustive, we can mention the codification and development of international law, the establishment of international norms regarding human rights, advances in humanitarian law, the resolution of numerous conflicts, operations of peace-keeping and reconciliation, and any number of other accomplishments in every area of international activity and endeavour. All these achievements are lights which help to dispel the darkness of the disorder caused by unrestrained ambitions and collective forms of selfishness. Certainly, many grave problems remain to be resolved, yet it is also clear that, without all this international activity, mankind would not have been able to survive the unchecked use of its own possibilities. Every one of these political, juridical and technical advances is a path towards attaining the ideal of human fraternity and a means for its greater realization.

I also pay homage to all those men and women whose loyalty and self-sacrifice have benefitted humanity as a whole in these past seventy years. In particular, I would recall today those who gave their lives for peace and reconciliation among peoples, from Dag Hammarskjöld to the many United Nations officials at every level who have been killed in the course of humanitarian missions, and missions of peace and reconciliation.

Beyond these achievements, the experience of the past seventy years has made it clear that reform and adaptation to the times is always necessary in the pursuit of the ultimate goal of granting all countries, without exception, a share in, and a genuine and equitable influence on, decision-making processes. The need for greater equity is especially true in the case of those bodies with effective executive capability, such as the Security Council, the Financial Agencies and the groups or mechanisms specifically created to deal with economic crises. This will help limit every kind of abuse or usury, especially where developing countries are concerned. The International Financial Agencies are should care for the sustainable development of countries and should ensure that they are not subjected to oppressive lending systems which, far from promoting progress, subject people to mechanisms which generate greater poverty, exclusion and dependence.

The work of the United Nations, according to the principles set forth in the Preamble and the first Articles of its founding Charter, can be seen as the development and promotion of the rule of law, based on the realization that justice is an essential condition for achieving the ideal of universal fraternity. In this context, it is helpful to recall that the limitation of power is an idea implicit in the concept of law itself. To give to each his own, to cite the classic definition of justice, means that no human individual or group can consider itself absolute, permitted to bypass the dignity and the rights of other individuals or their social groupings. The effective distribution of power (political, economic, defense-related, technological, etc.) among a plurality of subjects, and the creation of a juridical system for regulating claims and interests, are one concrete way of limiting power. Yet today's world presents us with many false rights and – at the same time – broad sectors which are vulnerable, victims of power badly exercised: for example, the natural environment and the vast ranks of the excluded. These sectors are closely interconnected and made increasingly fragile by dominant political and economic relationships. That is why their rights must be forcefully affirmed, by working to protect the environment and by putting an end to exclusion.

First, it must be stated that a true "right of the environment" does exist, for two reasons. First, because we human beings are part of the environment. We live in communion with it, since the environment itself entails ethical limits which human activity must acknowledge and respect. Man, for all his remarkable gifts, which "are signs of a uniqueness which transcends the spheres of physics and biology" (*Laudato Si'*, 81), is at the same time a part of these spheres. He possesses a body shaped by physical, chemical and biological elements, and can only survive and develop if the ecological environment is favourable. Any harm done to the environment, therefore, is harm done to humanity. Second, because every creature, particularly a living creature, has an intrinsic value, in its existence, its life, its beauty and its interdependence with other creatures. We Christians, together with the other monotheistic religions, believe that the universe is the fruit of a loving decision by the Creator, who permits man respectfully to use creation for the good of his fellow men and for the glory of the Creator; he is not authorized to abuse it, much less to destroy it. In all religions, the environment is a fundamental good (cf. ibid.).

The misuse and destruction of the environment are also accompanied by a relentless process of exclusion. In effect, a selfish and boundless thirst for power and material prosperity leads both to the misuse of available natural resources and to the exclusion of the weak and disadvantaged, either because they are differently abled (handicapped), or because they lack adequate information and technical expertise, or are incapable of decisive political action. Economic and social exclusion is a complete denial of human fraternity and a grave offense against human rights and the environment. The poorest are those who suffer most from such offenses, for three serious reasons: they are cast off by society, forced to live off what is discarded and suffer unjustly from the abuse of the environment. They are part of today's widespread and quietly growing "culture of waste".

The dramatic reality this whole situation of exclusion and inequality, with its evident effects, has led me, in union with the entire Christian people and many others, to take stock of my grave responsibility in this regard and to speak out, together with all those who are seeking urgently-needed and effective solutions. The adoption of the *2030 Agenda for Sustainable Development* at the World Summit, which opens today, is an important sign of hope. I am similarly confident that the *Paris Conference on Climatic Change* will secure fundamental and effective agreements.

Solemn commitments, however, are not enough, although they are certainly a necessary step toward solutions. The classic definition of justice which I mentioned earlier contains as one of its essential elements a constant and perpetual will: *Iustitia est constans et perpetua voluntas ius sum cuique tribuendi.* Our world demands of all government leaders a will which is effective, practical and constant, concrete steps and immediate measures for preserving and improving the natural environment and thus putting an end as quickly as possible to the phenomenon of social and economic exclusion, with its baneful consequences: human trafficking, the marketing of human organs and tissues, the sexual exploitation of boys and girls, slave labour, including prostitution, the drug and weapons trade, terrorism and international organized crime. Such is the magnitude of these situations and their toll in innocent lives, that we must avoid every temptation to fall into a declarationist nominalism which would assuage our consciences. We need to ensure that our institutions are truly effective in the struggle against all these scourges.

The number and complexity of the problems require that we possess technical instruments of verification. But this involves two risks. We can rest content with the bureaucratic exercise of drawing up long lists of good proposals – goals, objectives and statistics – or we can think that a single theoretical and aprioristic solution will provide an answer to all the challenges. It must never be forgotten that political and economic activity is only effective when it is understood as a prudential activity, guided by a perennial concept of justice and constantly conscious of the fact that, above and beyond our plans and programmes, we are dealing with real men and women who live, struggle and suffer, and are often forced to live in great poverty, deprived of all rights.

To enable these real men and women to escape from extreme poverty, we must allow them to be dignified agents of their own destiny. Integral human development and the full exercise of human dignity cannot be imposed. They must be built up and allowed to unfold for each individual, for every family, in communion with others, and in a right relationship with all those areas in which human social life develops – friends, communities, towns and cities, schools, businesses and unions, provinces, nations, etc. This presupposes and requires the right to education – also for girls (excluded in certain places) – which is ensured first and foremost by respecting and reinforcing the primary right of the family to educate its children, as well as the right of churches and social groups to support and assist families in the education of their children. Education conceived in this way is the basis for the implementation of the *2030 Agenda* and for reclaiming the environment.

At the same time, government leaders must do everything possible to ensure that all can have the minimum spiritual and material means needed to live in dignity and to create and support a family, which is the primary cell of any social development. In practical terms, this absolute minimum has three names: lodging, labour, and land; and one spiritual name: spiritual freedom, which includes religious freedom, the right to education and all other civil rights.

For all this, the simplest and best measure and indicator of the implementation of the new *Agenda* for development will be effective, practical and immediate access, on the part of all, to essential material and spiritual goods: housing, dignified and properly remunerated employment, adequate food and drinking water; religious freedom and, more generally, spiritual freedom and education. These pillars of integral human development have a common foundation, which is the right to life and, more generally, what we could call the right to existence of human nature itself.

The ecological crisis, and the large-scale destruction of biodiversity, can threaten the very existence of the human species. The baneful consequences of an irresponsible mismanagement of the global economy, guided only by ambition for wealth and power, must serve as a summons to a forthright reflection on man: "man is not only a freedom which he creates for himself. Man does not create himself. He is spirit and will, but also nature" (Benedict XVI, *Address to the Bundestag*, 22 September 2011, cited in *Laudato Si'*, 6). Creation is compromised "where we ourselves have the final word... The misuse of creation begins when we no longer recognize any instance above ourselves, when we see nothing else but ourselves" (ID. *Address to the Clergy of the Diocese of Bolzano-Bressanone, 6 August 2008*, cited ibid.). Consequently, the defence of the environment and the fight against exclusion demand that we recognize a moral law written into human nature itself, one which includes the natural difference between man and woman (cf. *Laudato Si'*, 155), and absolute respect for life in all its stages and dimensions (cf. ibid., 123, 136).

Without the recognition of certain incontestable natural ethical limits and without the immediate implementation of those pillars of integral human development, the ideal of "saving succeeding generations from the scourge of war" (*Charter of the United Nations*, Preamble), and "promoting social progress and better standards of life in larger freedom" (ibid.), risks becoming an unattainable illusion, or, even worse, idle chatter which serves as a cover for all kinds of abuse and corruption, or for carrying out an ideological colonization by the imposition of anomalous models and lifestyles which are alien to people's identity and, in the end, irresponsible.

War is the negation of all rights and a dramatic assault on the environment. If we want true integral human development for all, we must work tirelessly to avoid war between nations and peoples.

To this end, there is a need to ensure the uncontested rule of law and tireless recourse to negotiation, mediation and arbitration, as proposed by the *Charter of the United Nations*, which constitutes truly a fundamental juridical norm. The experience of these seventy years since the founding of the United Nations in general, and in particular the experience of these first fifteen years of the third millennium, reveal both the effectiveness of the full application of international norms and the ineffectiveness of their lack of enforcement. When the *Charter of the United Nations* is respected and applied with transparency and sincerity, and without ulterior motives, as an obligatory reference point of justice and not as a means of masking spurious intentions, peaceful results will be obtained. When, on the other hand, the norm is considered simply as an instrument to be used whenever it proves favourable, and to be avoided when it is not, a true Pandora's box is opened, releasing uncontrollable forces which gravely harm defenceless populations, the cultural milieu and even the biological environment.

The Preamble and the first Article of the *Charter of the United Nations* set forth the foundations of the international juridical framework: peace, the pacific solution of disputes and the development of friendly relations between the nations. Strongly opposed to such statements, and in practice denying them, is the constant tendency to the proliferation of arms, especially weapons of mass distraction, such as nuclear weapons. An ethics and a law based on the threat of mutual destruction – and possibly the destruction of all mankind – are self-contradictory and an affront to the entire framework of the United Nations, which would end up as "nations united by fear and distrust". There is urgent need to work for a world free of nuclear weapons, in full application of the non-proliferation Treaty, in letter and spirit, with the goal of a complete prohibition of these weapons.

The recent agreement reached on the nuclear question in a sensitive region of Asia and the Middle East is proof of the potential of political good will and of law, exercised with sincerity, patience and constancy. I express my hope that this agreement will be lasting and efficacious, and bring forth the desired fruits with the cooperation of all the parties involved.

In this sense, hard evidence is not lacking of the negative effects of military and political interventions which are not coordinated between members of the international community. For this reason, while regretting to have to do so, I must renew my repeated appeals regarding to the painful situation of the entire Middle East, North Africa and other African countries, where Christians, together with other cultural or ethnic groups, and even members of the majority religion who have no desire to be caught up in hatred and folly, have been forced to witness the destruction of their places of worship, their cultural and religious heritage, their houses and property, and have faced the alternative either of fleeing or of paying for their adhesion to good and to peace by their own lives, or by enslavement.

These realities should serve as a grave summons to an examination of conscience on the part of those charged with the conduct of international affairs. Not only in cases of religious or cultural persecution, but in every situation of conflict, as in Ukraine, Syria, Iraq, Libya, South Sudan and the Great Lakes region, real human beings take precedence over partisan interests, however legitimate the latter may be. In wars and conflicts there are individual persons, our brothers and sisters, men and women, young and old, boys and girls who weep, suffer and die. Human beings who are easily discarded when our response is simply to draw up lists of problems, strategies and disagreements.

As I wrote in my letter to the Secretary-General of the United Nations on 9 August 2014, "the most basic understanding of human dignity compels the international community, particularly through the norms and mechanisms of international law, to do all that it can to stop and to prevent further systematic violence against ethnic and religious minorities" and to protect innocent peoples.

Along the same lines I would mention another kind of conflict which is not always so open, yet is silently killing millions of people. Another kind of war experienced by many of our societies as a result of the narcotics trade. A war which is taken for granted and poorly fought. Drug trafficking is by its very nature accompanied by trafficking in persons, money laundering, the arms trade, child exploitation and other forms of corruption. A corruption which has penetrated to different levels of social, political, military, artistic and religious life, and, in many cases, has given rise to a parallel structure which threatens the credibility of our institutions.

I began this speech recalling the visits of my predecessors. I would hope that my words will be taken above all as a continuation of the final words of the address of Pope Paul VI; although spoken almost exactly fifty years ago, they remain ever timely. I quote: "The hour has come when a pause, a moment of recollection, reflection, even of prayer, is absolutely needed so that we may think back over our common origin, our history, our common destiny. The appeal to the moral conscience of man has never been as necessary as it is today... For the danger comes neither from progress nor from science; if these are used well, they can help to solve a great number of the serious problems besetting mankind (*Address to the United Nations Organization*, 4 October 1965). Among other things, human genius, well applied, will surely help to meet the grave challenges of ecological deterioration and of exclusion. As Paul VI said: "The real danger comes from man, who has at his disposal ever more powerful instruments that are as well fitted to bring about ruin as they are to achieve lofty conquests" (ibid.).

The common home of all men and women must continue to rise on the foundations of a right understanding of universal fraternity and respect for the sacredness of every human life, of every man and every woman, the poor, the elderly, children, the infirm, the unborn, the unemployed, the abandoned, those considered disposable because they are only considered as part of a statistic. This common home of all men and women must also be built on the understanding of a certain sacredness of created nature.

Such understanding and respect call for a higher degree of wisdom, one which accepts transcendence, self-transcendence, rejects the creation of an all-powerful élite, and recognizes that the full meaning of individual and collective life is found in selfless service to others and in the sage and respectful use of creation for the common good. To repeat the words of Paul VI, "the edifice of modern civilization has to be built on spiritual principles, for they are the only ones capable not only of supporting it, but of shedding light on it" (ibid.).

El Gaucho Martín Fierro, a classic of literature in my native land, says: "Brothers should stand by each other, because this is the first law; keep a true bond between you always, at every time – because if you fight among yourselves, you'll be devoured by those outside".

The contemporary world, so apparently connected, is experiencing a growing and steady social fragmentation, which places at risk "the foundations of social life" and consequently leads to "battles over conflicting interests" (*Laudato Si'*, 229).

The present time invites us to give priority to actions which generate new processes in society, so as to bear fruit in significant and positive historical events (cf. *Evangelii Gaudium*, 223). We cannot permit ourselves to postpone "certain agendas" for the future. The future demands of us critical and global decisions in the face of world-wide conflicts which increase the number of the excluded and those in need.

The praiseworthy international juridical framework of the United Nations Organization and of all its activities, like any other human endeavour, can be improved, yet it remains necessary; at the same time it can be the pledge of a secure and happy future for future generations. And so it will, if the representatives of the States can set aside partisan and ideological interests, and sincerely strive to serve the common good. I pray to Almighty God that this will be the case, and I assure you of my support and my prayers, and the support and prayers of all the faithful of the Catholic Church, that this Institution, all its member States, and each of its officials, will always render an effective service to mankind, a service respectful of diversity and capable of bringing out, for sake of the common good, the best in each people and in every individual. God bless you all. Thank you.

Visit to the joint session of the United States Congress

ADDRESS OF THE HOLY FATHER

United States Capitol, Washington, D.C.
Thursday, 24 September 2015

I am most grateful for your invitation to address this Joint Session of Congress in "the land of the free and the home of the brave". I would like to think that the reason for this is that I too am a son of this great continent, from which we have all received so much and toward which we share a common responsibility.

Each son or daughter of a given country has a mission, a personal and social responsibility. Your own responsibility as members of Congress is to enable this country, by your legislative activity, to grow as a nation. You are the face of its people, their representatives. You are called to defend and preserve the dignity of your fellow citizens in the tireless and demanding pursuit of the common good, for this is the chief aim of all politics. A political society endures when it seeks, as a vocation, to satisfy common needs by stimulating the growth of all its members, especially those in situations of greater vulnerability or risk. Legislative activity is always based on care for the people. To this you have been invited, called and convened by those who elected you.

Yours is a work which makes me reflect in two ways on the figure of Moses. On the one hand, the patriarch and lawgiver of the people of Israel symbolizes the need of peoples to keep alive their sense of unity by means of just legislation. On the other, the figure of Moses leads us directly to God and thus to the transcendent dignity of the human being. Moses provides us with a good synthesis of your work: you are asked to protect, by means of the law, the image and likeness fashioned by God on every human face.

Today I would like not only to address you, but through you the entire people of the United States. Here, together with their representatives, I would like to take this opportunity to dialogue with the many thousands of men and women who strive each day to do an honest day's work, to bring home their daily bread, to save money and –one step at a time – to build a better life for their families. These are men and women who are not concerned simply with paying their taxes, but in their own quiet way sustain the life of society. They generate solidarity by their actions, and they create organizations which offer a helping hand to those most in need.

I would also like to enter into dialogue with the many elderly persons who are a storehouse of wisdom forged by experience, and who seek in many ways, especially through volunteer work, to share their stories and their insights. I know that many of them are retired, but still active; they keep working to build up this land. I also want to dialogue with all those young people who are working to realize their great and noble aspirations, who are not led astray by facile proposals, and who face difficult situations, often as a result of immaturity on the part of many adults. I wish to dialogue with all of you, and I would like to do so through the historical memory of your people.

My visit takes place at a time when men and women of good will are marking the anniversaries of several great Americans. The complexities of history and the reality of human weakness notwithstanding, these men and women, for all their many differences and limitations, were able by hard work and self-sacrifice – some at the cost of their lives – to build a better future. They shaped fundamental values which will endure forever in the spirit of the American people. A people with this spirit can live through many crises, tensions and conflicts, while always finding the resources to move forward, and to do so with dignity. These men and women offer us a way of seeing and interpreting reality. In honoring their memory, we are inspired, even amid conflicts, and in the here and now of each day, to draw upon our deepest cultural reserves.

I would like to mention four of these Americans: Abraham Lincoln, Martin Luther King, Dorothy Day and Thomas Merton.

This year marks the one hundred and fiftieth anniversary of the assassination of President Abraham Lincoln, the guardian of liberty, who labored tirelessly that "this nation, under God, [might] have a new birth of freedom". Building a future of freedom requires love of the common good and cooperation in a spirit of subsidiarity and solidarity.

All of us are quite aware of, and deeply worried by, the disturbing social and political situation of the world today. Our world is increasingly a place of violent conflict, hatred and brutal atrocities, committed even in the name of God and of religion. We know that no religion is immune from forms of individual delusion or ideological extremism. This means that we must be especially attentive to every type of fundamentalism, whether religious or of any other kind. A delicate balance is required to combat violence perpetrated in the name of a religion, an ideology or an economic system, while also safeguarding religious freedom, intellectual freedom and individual freedoms. But there is another temptation which we must especially guard against: the simplistic reductionism which sees only good or evil; or, if you will, the righteous and sinners. The contemporary world, with its open wounds which affect so many of our brothers and sisters, demands that we confront every form of polarization which would divide it into these two camps. We know that in the attempt to be freed of the enemy without, we can be tempted to feed the enemy within. To imitate the hatred and violence of tyrants and murderers is the best way to take their place. That is something which you, as a people, reject.

Our response must instead be one of hope and healing, of peace and justice. We are asked to summon the courage and the intelligence to resolve today's many geopolitical and economic crises. Even in the developed world, the effects of unjust structures and actions are all too apparent. Our efforts must aim at restoring hope, righting wrongs, maintaining commitments, and thus promoting the well-being of individuals and of peoples. We must move forward together, as one, in a renewed spirit of fraternity and solidarity, cooperating generously for the common good.

The challenges facing us today call for a renewal of that spirit of cooperation, which has accomplished so much good throughout the history of the United States. The complexity, the gravity and the urgency of these challenges demand that we pool our resources and talents, and resolve to support one another, with respect for our differences and our convictions of conscience.

In this land, the various religious denominations have greatly contributed to building and strengthening society. It is important that today, as in the past, the voice of faith continue to be heard, for it is a voice of fraternity and love, which tries to bring out the best in each person and in each society. Such cooperation is a powerful resource in the battle to eliminate new global forms of slavery, born of grave injustices which can be overcome only through new policies and new forms of social consensus.

Here I think of the political history of the United States, where democracy is deeply rooted in the mind of the American people. All political activity must serve and promote the good of the human person and be based on respect for his or her dignity. "We hold these truths to be self-evident, that all men are created equal, that they are endowed by their Creator with certain unalienable rights, that among these are life, liberty and the pursuit of happiness" (*Declaration of Independence*, 4 July 1776). If politics must truly be at the service of the human person, it follows that it cannot be a slave to the economy and finance. Politics is, instead, an expression of our compelling need to live as one, in order to build as one the greatest common good: that of a community which sacrifices particular interests in order to share, in justice and peace, its goods, its interests, its social life. I do not underestimate the difficulty that this involves, but I encourage you in this effort.

Here too I think of the march which Martin Luther King led from Selma to Montgomery fifty years ago as part of the campaign to fulfill his "dream" of full civil and political rights for African Americans. That dream continues to inspire us all. I am happy that America continues to be, for many, a land of "dreams". Dreams which lead to action, to participation, to commitment. Dreams which awaken what is deepest and truest in the life of a people.

In recent centuries, millions of people came to this land to pursue their dream of building a future in freedom. We, the people of this continent, are not fearful of foreigners, because most of us were once foreigners. I say this to you as the son of immigrants, knowing that so many of you are also descended from immigrants. Tragically, the rights of those who were here long before us were not always respected. For those peoples and their nations, from the heart of American democracy, I wish to reaffirm my highest esteem and appreciation. Those first contacts were often turbulent and violent, but it is difficult to judge the past by the criteria of the present. Nonetheless, when the stranger in our midst appeals to us, we must not repeat the sins and the errors of the past. We must resolve now to live as nobly and as justly as possible, as we educate new generations not to turn their back on our "neighbors" and everything around us. Building a nation calls us to recognize that we must constantly relate to others, rejecting a mindset of hostility in order to adopt one of reciprocal subsidiarity, in a constant effort to do our best. I am confident that we can do this.

Our world is facing a refugee crisis of a magnitude not seen since the Second World War. This presents us with great challenges and many hard decisions. On this continent, too, thousands of persons are led to travel north in search of a better life for themselves and for their loved ones, in search of greater opportunities. Is this not what we want for our own children? We must not be taken aback by their numbers, but rather view them as persons, seeing their faces and listening to their stories, trying to respond as best we can to their situation. To respond in a way which is always humane, just and fraternal. We need to avoid a common temptation nowadays: to discard whatever proves troublesome. Let us remember the Golden Rule: "Do unto others as you would have them do unto you" (*Mt* 7:12).

This Rule points us in a clear direction. Let us treat others with the same passion and compassion with which we want to be treated. Let us seek for others the same possibilities which we seek for ourselves. Let us help others to grow, as we would like to be helped ourselves. In a word, if we want security, let us give security; if we want life, let us give life; if we want opportunities, let us provide opportunities. The yardstick we use for others will be the yardstick which time will use for us. The Golden Rule also reminds us of our responsibility to protect and defend human life at every stage of its development.

This conviction has led me, from the beginning of my ministry, to advocate at different levels for the global abolition of the death penalty. I am convinced that this way is the best, since every life is sacred, every human person is endowed with an inalienable dignity, and society can only benefit from the rehabilitation of those convicted of crimes. Recently my brother bishops here in the United States renewed their call for the abolition of the death penalty. Not only do I support them, but I also offer encouragement to all those who are convinced that a just and necessary punishment must never exclude the dimension of hope and the goal of rehabilitation.

In these times when social concerns are so important, I cannot fail to mention the Servant of God Dorothy Day, who founded the *Catholic Worker Movement*. Her social activism, her passion for justice and for the cause of the oppressed, were inspired by the Gospel, her faith, and the example of the saints.

How much progress has been made in this area in so many parts of the world! How much has been done in these first years of the third millennium to raise people out of extreme poverty! I know that you share my conviction that much more still needs to be done, and that in times of crisis and economic hardship a spirit of global solidarity must not be lost. At the same time I would encourage you to keep in mind all those people around us who are trapped in a cycle of poverty. They too need to be given hope. The fight against poverty and hunger must be fought constantly and on many fronts, especially in its causes. I know that many Americans today, as in the past, are working to deal with this problem.

It goes without saying that part of this great effort is the creation and distribution of wealth. The right use of natural resources, the proper application of technology and the harnessing of the spirit of enterprise are essential elements of an economy which seeks to be modern, inclusive and sustainable. "Business is a noble vocation, directed to producing wealth and improving the world. It can be a fruitful source of prosperity for the area in which it operates, especially if it sees the creation of jobs as an essential part of its service to the common good" (*Laudato Si'*, 129). This common good also includes the earth, a central theme of the encyclical which I recently wrote in order to "enter into dialogue with all people about our common home" (ibid., 3). "We need a conversation which includes everyone, since the environmental challenge we are undergoing, and its human roots, concern and affect us all" (ibid., 14).

In *Laudato Si'*, I call for a courageous and responsible effort to "redirect our steps" (ibid., 61), and to avert the most serious effects of the environmental deterioration caused by human activity. I am convinced that we can make a difference and I have no doubt that the United States – and this Congress – have an important role to play. Now is the time for courageous actions and strategies, aimed at implementing a "culture of care" (ibid., 231) and "an integrated approach to combating poverty, restoring dignity to the excluded, and at the same time protecting nature" (ibid., 139). "We have the freedom needed to limit and direct technology" (ibid., 112); "to devise intelligent ways of... developing and limiting our power" (ibid., 78); and to put technology "at the service of another type of progress, one which is healthier, more human, more social, more integral" (ibid., 112). In this regard, I am confident that America's outstanding academic and research institutions can make a vital contribution in the years ahead.

A century ago, at the beginning of the Great War, which Pope Benedict XV termed a "pointless slaughter", another notable American was born: the Cistercian monk Thomas Merton. He remains a source of spiritual inspiration and a guide for many people. In his autobiography he wrote: "I came into the world. Free by nature, in the image of God, I was nevertheless the prisoner of my own violence and my own selfishness, in the image of the world into which I was born. That world was the picture of Hell, full of men like myself, loving God, and yet hating him; born to love him, living instead in fear of hopeless self-contradictory hungers". Merton was above all a man of prayer, a thinker who challenged the certitudes of his time and opened new horizons for souls and for the Church. He was also a man of dialogue, a promoter of peace between peoples and religions.

From this perspective of dialogue, I would like to recognize the efforts made in recent months to help overcome historic differences linked to painful episodes of the past. It is my duty to build bridges and to help all men and women, in any way possible, to do the same. When countries which have been at odds resume the path of dialogue – a dialogue which may have been interrupted for the most legitimate of reasons – new opportunities open up for all. This has required, and requires, courage and daring, which is not the same as irresponsibility. A good political leader is one who, with the interests of all in mind, seizes the moment in a spirit of openness and pragmatism. A good political leader always opts to initiate processes rather than possessing spaces (cf. *Evangelii Gaudium*, 222-223).

Being at the service of dialogue and peace also means being truly determined to minimize and, in the long term, to end the many armed conflicts throughout our world. Here we have to ask ourselves: Why are deadly weapons being sold to those who plan to inflict untold suffering on individuals and society? Sadly, the answer, as we all know, is simply for money: money that is drenched in blood, often innocent blood. In the face of this shameful and culpable silence, it is our duty to confront the problem and to stop the arms trade.

Three sons and a daughter of this land, four individuals and four dreams: Lincoln, liberty; Martin Luther King, liberty in plurality and non-exclusion; Dorothy Day, social justice and the rights of persons; and Thomas Merton, the capacity for dialogue and openness to God.

Four representatives of the American people.

I will end my visit to your country in Philadelphia, where I will take part in the World Meeting of Families. It is my wish that throughout my visit the family should be a recurrent theme. How essential the family has been to the building of this country! And how worthy it remains of our support and encouragement! Yet I cannot hide my concern for the family, which is threatened, perhaps as never before, from within and without. Fundamental relationships are being called into question, as is the very basis of marriage and the family. I can only reiterate the importance and, above all, the richness and the beauty of family life.

In particular, I would like to call attention to those family members who are the most vulnerable, the young. For many of them, a future filled with countless possibilities beckons, yet so many others seem disoriented and aimless, trapped in a hopeless maze of violence, abuse and despair. Their problems are our problems. We cannot avoid them. We need to face them together, to talk about them and to seek effective solutions rather than getting bogged down in discussions. At the risk of oversimplifying, we might say that we live in a culture which pressures young people not to start a family, because they lack possibilities for the future. Yet this same culture presents others with so many options that they too are dissuaded from starting a family.

A nation can be considered great when it defends liberty as Lincoln did, when it fosters a culture which enables people to "dream" of full rights for all their brothers and sisters, as Martin Luther King sought to do; when it strives for justice and the cause of the oppressed, as Dorothy Day did by her tireless work, the fruit of a faith which becomes dialogue and sows peace in the contemplative style of Thomas Merton.

In these remarks I have sought to present some of the richness of your cultural heritage, of the spirit of the American people. It is my desire that this spirit continue to develop and grow, so that as many young people as possible can inherit and dwell in a land which has inspired so many people to dream.

God bless America!

Charlemagne Prize speech (EU)

Vatican, Sala Regia Friday, 6 May 2016

Creativity, genius and a capacity for rebirth and renewal are part of the soul of Europe. In the last century, Europe bore witness to humanity that a new beginning was indeed possible. After years of tragic conflicts, culminating in the most horrific war ever known, there emerged, by God's grace, something completely new in human history. The ashes of the ruins could not extinguish the ardent hope and the quest of solidarity that inspired the founders of the European project. They laid the foundations for a bastion of peace, an edifice made up of states united not by force but by free commitment to the *common good* and a definitive end to confrontation. Europe, so long divided, finally found its true self and began to build its house.

...

In addressing the European Parliament, I used the image of Europe as a grandmother. I noted that there is a growing impression that Europe is weary, aging, no longer fertile and vital, that the great ideals that inspired Europe seem to have lost their appeal. There is an impression that Europe is declining, that it has lost its ability to be innovative and creative, and that it is more concerned with preserving and dominating spaces than with generating processes of inclusion and change. There is an impression that Europe is tending to become increasingly "entrenched", rather than open to initiating new social processes capable of engaging all individuals and groups in the search for new and productive solutions to current problems. Europe, rather than protecting spaces, is called to be a mother who generates processes (cf. Apostolic Exhortation *Evangelii Gaudium*, 223).

Robert Schuman, at the very birth of the first European community, stated that "Europe will not be made all at once, or according to a single plan. It will be built through concrete achievements which first create a *de facto* solidarity".[3] Today, in our own world, marked by so much conflict and suffering, there is a need to return to the same *de facto solidarity* and *concrete generosity* that followed the Second World War, because, as Schuman noted, "world peace cannot be safeguarded without making creative efforts proportionate to the dangers threatening it".[4] The founding fathers were heralds of peace and prophets of the future. Today more than ever, their vision inspires us to build bridges and tear down walls. That vision urges us not to be content with cosmetic retouches or convoluted compromises aimed at correcting this or that treaty, but courageously to lay new and solid foundations. As Alcide De Gasperi stated, "equally inspired by concern for the common good of our European homeland", all are called to embark fearlessly on a "construction project that demands our full quota of patience and our ongoing cooperation".[5

Lately I have given much thought to this. I ask myself: How we can involve our young people in this building project if we fail to offer them employment, dignified labour that lets them grow and develop through their handiwork, their intelligence and their abilities? How can we tell them that they are protagonists, when the levels of employment and underemployment of millions of young Europeans are continually rising? How can we avoid losing our young people, who end up going elsewhere in search of their dreams and a sense of belonging, because here, in their own countries, we don't know how to offer them opportunities and values?

The just distribution of the fruits of the earth and human labour is not mere philanthropy. It is a moral obligation.[7] If we want to rethink our society, we need to create dignified and well-paying jobs, especially for our young people.

To do so requires coming up with new, more inclusive and equitable economic models, aimed not at serving the few, but at benefiting ordinary people and society as a whole. This calls for moving from a liquid economy to a social economy; I think for example of the social market economy encouraged by my predecessors (cf. JOHN PAUL II, *Address to the Ambassador of the Federal Republic of Germany*, 8 November 1990). It would involve passing from an economy directed at revenue, profiting from speculation and lending at interest, to a social economy that invests in persons by creating jobs and providing training.

We need to move from a liquid economy prepared to use corruption as a means of obtaining profits to a social economy that guarantees access to land and lodging through labour. Labour is in fact the setting in which individuals and communities bring into play "many aspects of life: creativity, planning for the future, developing talents, living out values, relating to others, giving glory to God. It follows that, in the reality of today's global society, it is essential that we 'continue to prioritize the role of access to steady employment for everyone, no matter the limited interests of business and dubious economic reasoning'[8]" (Encyclical *Laudato Si'*, 127).

If we want a dignified future, a future of peace for our societies, we will only be able to achieve it by working for genuine inclusion, "an inclusion which provides worthy, free, creative, participatory and solidary work".[9] This passage (from a liquid economy to a social economy) will not only offer new prospects and concrete opportunities for integration and inclusion, but will makes us once more capable of envisaging that humanism of which Europe has been the *cradle and wellspring*.

With mind and heart, with hope and without vain nostalgia, like a son who rediscovers in Mother Europe his roots of life and faith, I dream of a *new European humanism*, one that involves "a constant work of humanization" and calls for "memory, courage, [and] a sound and humane utopian vision".[10] I dream of a Europe that is young, still capable of being a mother: a mother who has life because she respects life and offers hope for life. I dream of a Europe that cares for children, that offers fraternal help to the poor and those newcomers seeking acceptance because they have lost everything and need shelter. I dream of a Europe that is attentive to and concerned for the infirm and the elderly, lest they be simply set aside as useless. I dream of a Europe where being a migrant is not a crime but a summons to greater commitment on behalf of the dignity of every human being. I dream of a Europe where young people breathe the pure air of honesty, where they love the beauty of a culture and a simple life undefiled by the insatiable needs of consumerism, where getting married and having children is a responsibility and a great joy, not a problem due to the lack of stable employment. I dream of a Europe of families, with truly effective policies concentrated on faces rather than numbers, on birth rates more than rates of consumption. I dream of a Europe that promotes and protects the rights of everyone, without neglecting its duties towards all. I dream of a Europe of which it will not be said that its commitment to human rights was its last utopia. Thank you.

Laudato Si and Romano Guardini
Fr. Robert Barron

In 1986, after serving in a variety of capacities in the Jesuit province of Argentina, Jorge Mario Bergoglio commenced doctoral studies in Germany. The focus of his research was the great twentieth century theologian and cultural critic Romano Guardini, who had been a key influence on, among many others, Karl Rahner, Henri de Lubac, and Joseph Ratzinger. As things turned out, Bergoglio never finished his doctoral degree (he probably started too late in life), but his immersion in the writings of Guardini decisively shaped his thinking. Most of the commentary on Pope Francis's encyclical *Laudato Si'* has focused on the issue of global warming and the Pope's alignment with this or that political perspective, but this is to miss the forest for one very particular tree. As I read through the document, I saw, on practically every page, the influence of Romano Guardini and his distinctive take on modernity.

To get a handle on Guardini's worldview, one should start with a series of essays that he wrote in the 1920's, gathered into book form as _Letters from Lake Como_. Like many Germans (despite his very Italian name, Guardini was culturally German), he loved to vacation in Italy, and he took particular delight in the lake region around Milan. He was enchanted, of course, by the physical beauty of the area, but what intrigued him above all was the manner in which human beings, through their architecture and craftsmanship, interacted non-invasively and respectfully with nature. When he first came to the region, he noticed, for example, how the homes along Lake Como imitated the lines and rhythms of the landscape and how the boats that plied the lake did so in response to the swelling and falling of the waves. But by the 1920's, he had begun to notice a change. The homes being built were not only larger, but more "aggressive," indifferent to the surrounding environment, no longer accommodating themselves to the natural setting. And the motor-driven boats on the lake were no longer moving in rhythm with the waves, but rather cutting through them indifferently.

In these unhappy changes, Guardini noted the emergence of a distinctively modern sensibility. He meant that the attitudes first articulated by Francis Bacon in the sixteenth century and René Descartes in the seventeenth were coming to dominate the mentality of twentieth-century men and women. Consciously departing from Aristotle, who had said that knowledge is a modality of contemplation, Bacon opined that knowledge is power, more precisely power to control the natural environment. This is why he infamously insisted that the scientist's task is to put nature "on the rack" so that she might give up her secrets. Just a few decades later, Descartes told the intellectuals of Europe to stop fussing over theological matters and philosophical abstractions and to get about the business of "mastering" nature. To be sure, this shift in consciousness gave rise to the modern sciences and their attendant technologies, but it also, Guardini worried, led to a deep alienation between humanity and nature. The typically modern subject became aggressive and self-absorbed, and the natural world simply something for him to manipulate for his own purposes.

If you want to see an English version of Guardini's perspective, I would recommend a careful reading of C.S. Lewis, J.R.R. Tolkien, and their Inklings colleagues on the relation between capitalist, technocratic humanity and an increasingly aggressed nature. If you want vivid images for this, turn to the pages in *The Lord of the Rings* dealing with the battle between Saruman and the Ents or to the section of *The Lion, the Witch, and the Wardrobe* detailing the permanent winter into which Narnia had fallen.

It is only against this Guardinian background that we can properly read the Pope's latest encyclical. Whatever his views on global warming, they are situated within the far greater context of a theology of nature that stands athwart the typically modern point of view. That the earth has become "piled with filth," that pollution adversely affects the health of millions of the poor, that we live in a "throwaway" culture, that the unborn are treated with indifference, that huge populations have little access to clean drinking water, that thousands of animal species are permitted to fall into extinction, and yes even that we live in housing that bears no organic relation to the natural environment—all of it flows from the alienated Cartesian subject going about his work of mastering nature. In the spirit of the author of the book of Genesis, the Biblical prophets, Irenaeus, Thomas Aquinas, Francis of Assisi—indeed of any great pre-modern figure—Pope Francis wants to recover a properly cosmological sensibility, whereby the human being and her projects are in vibrant, integrated relation with the world that surrounds her.

What strikes the Pope as self-evident is that the nature we have attempted to dominate, for the past several centuries, has now turned on us, like Frankenstein's monster. As he put it in a recent press conference, "God always forgives; human beings sometimes forgive; but when nature is mistreated, she never forgives." These lessons, which he learned many years ago from Romano Guardini, are still worthy of careful attention today.

Peace Building: Lessons from Assisi

Assisi Pax[103]

The mission of Assisi Pax International is to promote a viable project for peace. In our view, peace means a concrete proposal for the development of humankind's civilization rather than a utopian dream. We believe that peace is built by joint efforts step by step. For centuries, political, economic and spiritual leaders and the common people have called for peace without it being fully achieved. Thus today many people feel disheartened and think that peace will never be achieved on our planet. However, we believe that peace is possible through a change in our way of thinking and visualizing the world. As stated in *Gaudium and Spes*, peace is much more than the absence of war: it means developing positive rapport between all human beings and creatures. As a consequence, if we base our relationships on the assumption, inspired by the Bible, that there is something positive in each person, then we believe that we can create a pathway to peace.

Today armed conflicts and the power politics of economic domination prevail at all levels of human interaction and are viewed as normal behavior by mainstream culture. Under such a reality, peace can only be regarded as a temporary suspension of conflicts rather than a permanent state for humankind. In the context of a society in which conflict is normative, peace can only be seen as utopia. If we really want peace, then we have to change the context.

We think that new patterns of relationship can be established in the human family and between the human family and the natural world. St Francis set the example when he met the sultan Melek-el-Kamil. On that occasion he "invented" and brought *dialogue into the situation*, thus finding a solution to deep-rooted conflicts between Muslims and Christians that had seemed unsolvable until then.

Our commitment to a *Civilization of Peace* stems from our deep belief in dialogue. If we bring dialogue in any situation, then we can state that peace is possible and fruitful.

Dialogue and positive attitudes towards the other are the key to peace building and peace keeping.

WHAT IS A CIVILIZATION OF PEACE?
We should first answer these questions?
What is civilization?
What is peace?

Civilization
Simply put, civilization is made up of the network of relationships we have with every being: human beings, the natural world, God and with ourselves. It is through relationships that our individual and communal lives are based. Every society shares a set of values that constitute their civilization and are at the core of their living together. Any civilization has its own features and these different features are not to be seen as a source of conflicts but a source of strength. When civilizations are not in conflict, their diversity can be a driving force of

---

[103] Reference Assisi Pax

social cohesion and peace within a country and among countries. Diversity is not a cause of division but a source of richness.

Peace
Peace is much more than the absence of war. It is the process that starts once wars are over, hate has been quenched and tensions have been defused. Only then is the construction of peace possible, provided that a positive attitude is adopted towards every being and situation.In religious terms, peace (Biblical shalom, the same root as salaam in Arabic) is the reconstruction of the ancient harmony between humanity, creation and even death.
Ultimately, in Christian faith, peace is the final return to Eden, made possible after we have been redeemed by Christ.

Civilization of peace
Following what we have just said, peace does not consist in a generic wish for peace or some equally generic peace actions, like a flag waved on a march. Instead, peace is found in a "culture of the positive" that acknowledges and values the positive qualities of every human being. Also our relationships with any creature will be established on such a positive attitude.We are committed to building a civilization of peace whose strengths are putting our trust in positiveness and overcoming the concepts of enemy and conflict. This is what is learnt from the Christian reading of creation.

FAITH AND OTHER VIEWPOINTS
A note is necessary. When we speak about peace, we usually refer to the Christian faith and we use the language of that faith to convey our beliefs and proposals. Faith has its own language to read the world. We believe that the viewpoint of faith does not disagree with other complementary viewpoints, i.e., those of science and rational thinking. For this reason, religious language needs translating into the other languages that interpret the world.

The peace proposal of Assisi Pax International was conceived by Father GianMaria Polidoro out of his insights into interpreting St Francis's reading of the Gospel.

OUR PEACE COMMITMENT
Our commitment to peace stems first of all from a cultural change that entails:

- modifying our way of thinking and visualizing the world.
- speaking a "language of peace" which dismisses terms and expressions connected to the "language of conflict". Words like defeating, winning, enemy etc. recall conflict stances and maintain a culture of conflict;
- adopting a methodology of peace centred around dialogue which is based on the discovery and acknowledgment of the positiveness of the other;
- adopting nonviolence in the context of our society;
- making peace with creation;
- holding the strong conviction that peace is not only possible but also fruitful; and its fruitfulness should be the spur to our acting in society on our journey to peace.

Mission Assisi and CEFID (interfaith Peace Building) [104]

Interreligious dialogue

Written by Father Max Mizzi in May 2006

Inter-religious dialogue is a new movement in the Catholic Church and also in the other Christian Churches. Through the centuries no official dialogue existed between the many religions on earth - on the contrary. Their followers ignored each other and, indeed, they had numerous conflicts, wars and even persecuted each other. This they did sometimes in the name of God. Unfortunately that is also true to some extent even today. In our present year of 2006 we have in fact witnessed conflicts between Hindus and Christians in India and between Moslems and Christians in Sudan, Nigeria and other places.

The Second Vatican Council and the peace meeting in Assisi

In the Catholic Church the beginning of inter-religious dialogue is to be traced to *"the Second Vatican Council"* (1962-1965) especially with the Council Degree "Nostra Aetate" by which Catholics are encouraged to have positive relationships with the followers of the various religions particularly with the Jews and the Moslems, who are followers of the other monotheistic religions. In fact both the Muslims and the Jews adore, acknowledge and worship the same one God, as we Christians do.

The Council document makes reference also to the Hindus, to the Buddhists and to the other religions.

This opened a new horizon for the whole world and changed the attitude of the Catholic Church towards the other religions. It also changed for the better the relationship between the religions of the world. The followers of the different religions rather than ignore each other or persecute each other, now started to have a relationship of dialogue, friendship, respect and collaboration. With this Council document there was a sigh of relief not only among Catholics, but also among the other Christians and the followers of the world religions. When the Second Vatican Council was over the Catholic Church soon started to make contacts with the followers of the other religions. There was a very good response on all sides. It was like "tasting the waters" as we say. It was a timid initiative which lasted about twenty years until *"the World Day of Prayer for Peace"* was held in Assisi on 27th October 1986.

In fact we can say that inter-religious dialogue on a large scale and in practice started after the World Day of Prayer for Peace to which Pope John Paul II invited the representatives of the world religions to pray for peace in Assisi.

---

[104] From and See the CEFID and also Assisi Mission

After this historic event people started to talk about ***"inter-religious dialogue"*** and to, actually, have dialogue. In Assisi the concept of inter-religious dialogue came out into the light. It was not simply confined to a document any longer but it became a practice. After the meeting in Assisi inter-religious dialogue spread like wild fire all over the world. Many inter-religious talks and conferences were organized, and still are, in different parts of the world. The motive behind these meetings is to create a new spirit between the religions of the world, to bring the different religious leaders to talk with each other and to collaborate with each other in order to find new solutions to conflicts, to world poverty and injustice, to the safeguard of Creation, to eliminate violence against women and children and to encourage respect and love towards each other in the human family.

Following this new spirit numerous initiatives were taken. In 1988 the Global Forum of Spiritual and Political Leaders' conference was held in Oxford, England. Besides the Dalai Lama, Mother Teresa of Calcutta also participated. In 1993 in Chicago, USA, followed what was called the Parliament of the World Religions in which participated some three hundred religious leaders, politicians and scientists from many parts of the world including the Dalai Lama. The Parliament of the World Religions has met twice after the meeting in 1993, namely in Cape Town, South Africa and in Barcelona, Spain. Marking the New Millennium, in the year 2000, a big meeting of the world's religious leaders was held in New York, USA. This time it was at the United Nations. This was considered to be a recognition by the United Nations of the importance of inter-religious dialogue. It's difficult to say how many, and when, such various international meetings have been held, because they are numberless.

Such meetings can change the face of the world. They are perfect instruments of peace, collaboration and love. Conflicts must be solved not by violence, hatred and wars, but through sincere dialogue, respect and justice. Religious leaders or any individual must never use religion as an excuse for violence. That is against the very essence of religion and against God in whose name many conflicts are carried out, and is a serious crime against the human family.

Apart from these big international meetings many others not less important are held between different religious commissions and delegations such as Catholic and Jewish representatives, Hindu and Catholic delegations, meetings between Moslem and Christian delegates, or between Buddhist and monastic life representatives, and other forms of dialogue across previous barriers. These are mostly held on spiritual and theological topics such as prayer, meditation, the monastic life, and so on. Strict theological dialogue is still in the very early stages. It is easier for the religious leaders to talk about peace and injustice, spirituality and meditation for example, than to discuss God, redemption, eternal life and so on. But the way has also been opened to theological dialogue.

Because of the World Day of Prayer for Peace and the inter-religious dialogue that followed the prayer meeting of 1986, Assisi has become a place well known among the world religions. It is considered by the followers of all religions to be a very holy place. This is mainly because of St Francis who is the saint of peace and love, and he respected the whole of Creation. St Francis can rightly be considered the forerunner of inter-religious dialogue because of his meeting with the Moslems in the Middle East, especially with the Sultan of Egypt, Melek el Kamil, in 1219-20 during the 3rd Crusade. After the peace meeting in 1986, Assisi has been called *"Prophecy of Peace"*. Furthermore Pope John Paul II often referred to the *"Spirit of Assisi"*, which is the spirit of prayer, of peace and of dialogue.

The 'Spirit of Assisi" should not be confined only to associations or to religious leaders. Every individual man and woman is called to foster dialogue, understanding, respect, peace and love among the followers of religions. This should not be difficult especially in those countries where people from different cultures live together such as in many parts of Europe. It is very sad to see that many religious and social barriers still exist among people who live and work shoulder to shoulder. Many meetings and dialogues could be organized just on a small scale, in small groups of people from various cultures. It could be over a cup of tea or a meal for example. Such small groups can work wonders.

The world needs *instruments of peace and dialogue*, today's society needs *prophets of peace* and the religions of the word need *collaborators*.

Fr. Maximilian Mizzi OFM Conv.
Delegate for ecumenism and inter-religious dialogue at the Sacro
Convento and the Basilica of St. Francis, Assisi

2000 Year of Leadership (in Religion)

Ever since the start of the first Christian Church, debates, opinions and dialogues have been present on how to interpret and what it meant to live according to His example and God's life plan.

Where there is Light, unfortunately- and at times, there can also be Shadows or Darkness visiting the place.

The tales and stories of divisions, trespasses and of dominions- in and between the clergy and the men and women of faith or good will, and the Church, have been well documented, and are available for those who wishes to better understand the 2000 year young history from early Christianity to the sacred traditions protected and modernities in the Holy Church, today

So much is clear.[105]

But that is not what I like to speak about.

What I do like to speak about is that over the time of its' existence, the Church has have had it's healthy amount of Reforms and Reformists.

People who stood-up, were inspired, and felt called upon- to clarify the better interpretation or the better way of life – on the path of Christ

Let me mention you just here two examples – in the Church- and over a good period of time:

Saint Francis the Founder of the Order of Friars Minor (1209 AD), Ignatius of Loyala - the founder of the order of the Jesuits (1541 AD), and Saint Jose Maria of Opus Dei (1930)[106]

All of the above three founders were living in different times, different locations, and with different eyes and societal needs.

Franciscans

Saint Francis' call to reform was made in his direct relationship with his earthly father, and the ways by which he observed the Rich[107] treating the Poor in his days.

In deep suffering on such amount of injustice, the lack of true love and compassion among his people in Assisi (for Nature, animals, the poor), [108] made Francis see himself in prayer before the San Damiano Cross and hear the call from God:

---

[105] This is as valid for any religion, any faith, or any spiritual human development
[106] Opus Dei - today not free from scandal or concerns.
[107] Including his father
[108] the hang for wealth by the noble and clergy

"Francis- Go rebuild my Church"[109]

Well- the rest is history.

In 2013, when Cardinal Bergoglio was elected to become the new Pope and he made the decision to chose Saints Francis name for his Papacy ,

- and further re-inforced his choice in Pope Francis' encyclical Laudato Si ! [110]

- and the large attention and interests of 5 million pilgrims annually from all over the world to visit Assisi, Saint Francis' birthplace and tomb, including many holy churches and shrines

- makes that call quite alive.

"Francis- Go rebuild my Church".

Jesuits

Ignatius of Loayla, an Spanish (Rich) Nobleman, converted over a period of time, and actually was largely inspired by the lives and works of Saint Francis.

It was on 15 August 1534, at the age of 44, that Ignatius and his early disciples made their vow in the St Peters Church of Montmarte in Paris.

To serve God and to leave the things of the World behind

Go forth and set the world on fire

Two key duties were on their minds:

To counter the rise of Protestantism and to become the Educator (bringer) of "the good faith":

Ignatius "Spiritual Exercises" – a handbook of meditation, prayer and disciscipline- became core to the group and later group functions of the Jesuits.

[14] The main aim of the Exercises is the development of discernment (*discretio*), the ability to discern between good and evil spirits. A good "spirit" can bring love, joy, peace, but also desolation, to bring one to re-examine one's life. An evil spirit usually brings confusion, and doubt, but may also prompt contentment to discourage change. The human soul is continually drawn in two directions: towards goodness but at the same time towards sinfulness

As the key mission, function and objectives of the Jesuits was to become "the striker of" and for the Pope "on missionary work" (counter-reformist movement)

---

[109] Whilst Francis first interpreted this call from God too literally, his later ways of Life truly helped to reform and reshape the Living Church- as we can witness today in Pope Francis' name, Laudato Si! And in the Spirit of Assisi.

[110] Laudato Si! Is the name of one of the more famous poems (prayer) wirtten by Saint Francis

and to become the de-facto educator of "the good faith" in mission, schools and universities of the elite.

In this strategy and plans of the Jesuits, they saw themselves becoming quite of influence to the rise of good Catholic Christian Societies in the New World (Americas), as they became and were able to educate the key decision makers, politicians and elite of these societies.

In the 16th and 17th Century, the Jesuits had become an all powerful and influential group within the Catholic Church – with missionaries around the globe (Latin America)

At a certain moment in time, the Jesuits were believed to be the bankers of the America's, with key loans and possessions in the America's managed by their hands.

That, and some other mishaps or events of distrusts between the order and the Vatican, caused a period of redemption, and allowed the Jesuits to purify and modernize to what it is today:

The **Society of Jesus** (Latin: *Societas Iesu, S.J., SJ* or *SI*) is a male religious congregation of the Catholic Church. The members are called **Jesuits**. The society is engaged in evangelization and apostolic ministry in 112 nations on six continents. Jesuits work in education (founding schools, colleges, universities and seminaries), intellectual research, and cultural pursuits. Jesuits also give retreats, minister in hospitals and parishes, and promote social justice and ecumenical dialogue.

It may be observed here - that Pope Francis is from origin a Jesuit, and trained and well-educated Jesuit, and to that end- is quite familiar with the history and the reforms within this order.

Pope Francis is the first Jesuit ever to become Pope.

Opus Dei

In the early 20th Century, and again in Spain, a new phenomena is born.

Opus Dei (Work of God)

Or in other words:

Finding God in Daily Live and Work

It was Saint **Josemaría Escrivá de Balaguer** (9 January 1902 – 26 June 1975; also known as **Saint Josemaría, José María** or **Josemaría Escrivá de Balaguer y Albás**, born **José María Mariano Escriba Albás**[1]) was a Roman Catholic priest from Spain who founded Opus Dei, an organization of laypeople and priests dedicated to the teaching that everyone is called to holiness and that ordinary life is a path to sanctity. He was canonized in 2002 by Pope John Paul II, who declared Saint Josemaría should be "counted among the great witnesses of Christianity."[2][3]

===

A prayerful retreat helped him to further discern what he considered to be God's will for him, and, on 2 October 1928, he "saw" Opus Dei (English: Work of God), a way by which Catholics might learn to sanctify themselves through their secular work.[17] He founded it in 1928, and Pius XII gave it final approval in 1950. According to the decree of the Congregation for the Causes of Saints, which contains a condensed biography of Escrivá, "[t]o this mission he gave himself totally. From the beginning his was a very wide-ranging apostolate in social environments of all kinds.

Opus Dei was established in 1928 in Spain, and is today present in 66 countries, with approximately 100,000 followers.[111]

===

So- it is when we come to see - over history and time- ,that we may also better come to appreciate and sense the deeper mystery and wonder in the journey of religion, tradition and reform:

Firstly- the "story and thread" is that of deep respect, honor, preservation and perseverance of "what is good" ("the Story of Christ") over a remarkable period of time.

Secondly, the weaving of a "healthy reform, clarification, purification and attunement" of the early messages of "the good news" to the new times and needs people see or feel themselves in.

Thirdly, and let us never ever forget this- this is for and by the people

The combination makes up for a "Living Church".

The combination makes up for a Church of mystery and miracles of faith.

A Church which is ever under development with, by and for its' people.[112]

Of course. The Church has his more formal organization under the Popes and the Vatican, with Councils and Curia leading the mainstream of its' ways.

---

[111]

[112] And in atunement with the Most Highest, and Living Christ.

The Leadership of Pope John Paul II, the Second Vatican Council and the present leadership of the Holy See by Pope Francis are seen as other great reformists – in their times.

But that is not the point of this conversation.

The point of this conversation is that we may come to see what "a Living Church" or "Living Leadership" means and how it may become Three-in-One:

Honoring a Tradition, Reforming a Tradition – and by and for its' people.[113]

In a most caring way.

Three-in-One.

That, to my mind, is the mystery and art of "Living Leadership-Together" .

Well, 2000 years after the birth of Christ, and if we look ourselves in the mirror and look at what is around in our daily news- than I hope that you agree with me, that we still have some Living Leadership to do, together.

Go- and rebuild our World

---

[113] In and with Christ – in the Catholic religion.

Small Tales of Leadership Conversion in Business and Governments

Paris Agreement, UN Sustainable Development: The importance of Peace Building in Our Leadership Programs.

Peace is much more than the absence of war.

Peace is possible when we have created the calmer conditions and adopted a deep and shared positive attitude – *in community and in our relationships-* towards *every* being and situation.

The importance of this form of Peace in our Leadership, and Leadership over Change – in the Paris Agreement and the UN Sustainable Development Agenda and goals cannot be underestimated.

That I hope- I have made clear.

First of all- our modern, very busy and complex societies asks, begs an invites our political and business leadership- that can become stewards and Ambassadors of " Peace and All Good" in our own communities and societies.

Whilst we recognize that we live in a world with many people, with many views, many interest and perspectives on things- we may also recognize that for living together, well, we need Peace.

Peace within ourselves.

Peace between ourselves

Peace first in our own community, own company or own nation

And then in the relationship with other communities, other companies, and other nations.

(quote)

Every society shares a set of values that constitute their civilization and are at the core of their living together.

Any civilization has its own features and these different features are not to be seen as a source of conflicts but a source of strength. When civilizations are not in conflict, their diversity can be a driving force of social cohesion and peace within a country and among countries. Diversity is not a cause of division but a source of richness.

(unquote)

To build and lead this form of Peace needs patience, true compassion and care, atonement (to Peace) and ever more joyful, positive and free living.

Let me phrase it clear to you:

Unfortunately- there are very few places on Earth today, where there is this form of Peace.

This form of Peace cannot be there- where people are too busy, too occupied or have to run for or after their money, performances or (market) power and influences.

This form of Peace cannot be there if people are afraid or scared to lose their jobs, their income, their freedoms, or their ways of living.

This form of Peace cannot be there if there are wide diversities between the rich and the poor, the haves' and have not's

This form of Peace cannot be there if we are scared for the other, or we see ourselves in conflict with another race, nation, ethnicity, gender, and so on.

This form of Peace cannot be there if we worry about our daily food, our homes, our health, our safety, our etc.

This form of Peace cannot be there if we are scared for our thoughts, or our expressions of self in and within our societies. If we are afraid that we are not politically correct or accepted by the majority within our communities. Where compassion and care for "the diverse, the ones that are different or odd" are not taking place

This form of Peace cannot be there if our consuming habits and our lives are based on suffering by others: either in Nature or by other human beings.

This form of Peace cannot be there, if our ways of life are unsustainable, where we know that we borrow from our children, and indebt our future societies with poisons that cannot easily be healed.

This form of Peace cannot exist if we don't change our ways of how we see and experience our life's success: what is winning, and what is true peaceful living?

This form of Peace cannot exist if we still maintain to teach and educate our children and our employees that winning, competition and becoming first- in our nation, in our company and in our school- is that what matters most.

This form of Peace cannot exist if we compare our company, our country with others, and wish to see ourselves better, or exceptional, over the rest.

This form of Peace cannot exist, if we organize our work and life such that money becomes a prime source of objectives and in order to attain ourselves the opportunity to have a so-called free life, away from mainstream.

This form of Peace cannot exist, when we join large companies and government administrations, and where we are tasked to accomplish jobs and perform things that are incongruent with how we feel, think or believe in.

This form of Peace cannot exist if we are dominated by others, are owned or told by others what to think or do, and if we feel that our lives are taken away from us.

How can Peace exist if our world of work is called Busy-ness?

Busy-ness and Peace cannot walk hand-in-hand- if Busy-ness does not learn to appreciate and understand that Peace, Compassion and Joy with work, and monetary results and progression- are not each others enemy.

But without Peace and Compassion- nothing good can be build.

Peace and Compassion comes first,

That is what we are asked to learn and understand.

Peace asks us to see again and see to live with a deep and compassionate love and respect for every being

You can't fake that.

Peace ask for living wonderfully

Peace asks for calm and care

Peace asks us to re-imagine ourselves

The absence of this form of Peace, is the source of many conflict, frustrations and loss of life (and nature) around.

So- if we find our ways of building Peace, true Peace, then we may actually accomplish

And this form of Peace- requires first a conversation and conversion of ourselves.

Learning to Find our Ways

Two things I would like you to understand.:

The first thing:

When we engineered our present civilization, we *never* engineered it with our understanding that 9 billion people were going to use our inventions in these great intense production and consuming ways.

So- the "first weaving error" we have in our present human civilization, is that we have based our technological developments on local use numbers only.

We designed cars, houses, airplanes, super markets, entertainment, holidays, etc. etc. all based on what we could sell, market and develop in our local communities- the American or China Dream: step by step , stone by stone.

But now, and today, all these steps and all these stones- build over decades, has become quite a House of Cards (so to speak)

The present fundaments, or the Global House, are no longer fit for all these Dreams carried in our world.

Its' unfit to carry them.

Out of Sync.

Not engineered to do so.

The second thing I would like you to understand- is the following.

We can not change or safe the world, by saving the Climate.

We cannot deliver on the Paris Climate Change Agreement – if we cannot take care of Nature and Human Life.

Again- Pope Francis saw this so right with his Encyclical Laudato Si!

The Paris Climate Agreement is only *a derivative* of something more deeper, more essential we are invited to see and change.

With Pope Francis - I have come to see the need and care for a more integral ecology and human development, where social, ecological and economic principles no longer fight, but are in true harmony between themselves .

With Pope Francis, I have come to see in the natural order of things, and that things are best developed when they flow, are unfolded and created from loving kindness, care and compassion in all of our ways.

With Pope Francis, I share the sense that we are here for a higher meaning and our better selves come to speak , when we make ourselves available – truly available- to nature, our fellow man/woman and this call from our Creation[114]

Hence our best, and most is to raise our level of consciousness.

To disseminate, nurture and grow our level of awareness and atonement with the above.

As it is in this atonement, that we will find the answers too many of the complexities and calls for transformational change on our ways.

As it is in this atonement, that we will be able to assure ourselves, that our judgement on human development and economic progress is balanced, and is based from a good intent, source and will

As it is in this atonement, that we can assure ourselves, that even as the days may become hard, complex, demanding or challenging-

We find the answers that will make things more harmonic, more peaceful, better

Even if the aggregate of our human and economic development, or the day-to-day and ways of going about politics, international relationships, economy, sustainability, social justice, peace, etc. does not look good (in the newspapers, or in real) or is temporary out of sync,

We know, that in our atonement, we find the most essentials answers for our today and tomorrow.

What deserves our attention, what deserves a decision or action forwards.

Now- from where I am today, and where you may be today- I cannot expect you to agree or see this all with me.

On this, that or all.

---

[114] Common Home, Divine

But what *I do know* is that by so-called *running ourselves* in sustainability, and by blindly following what is today's (political/economic) agenda or o so many very urgent and important organizational initiatives and re-active fire-fighting and calls,

Is not helping to lead us our ways.

Leadership, true Stewardship over our Common Home, requires something else.

It asks for Soul.

It's not a gimmick. It's not something cool.

It's the real-deal.

The more honest and undeniable truth

You can't fake it. You can't make or mask it.

It is who you are and have allowed yourself to become.

Spiritual and religion leaders know it.

Great human development leaders (e.g. Ghandi, Mandela) know it.

Great (and true) Business Leadership may know it.-.

It's a path of ever more training, and making yourself available to be able to deliver on the more.

More complex. More demanding. More value and values making

Now- for today and tomorrow- we need true leaders that can engineer the UN Sustainable Development goals,

Not only in one company

Not only in one nation

But in between our nations and for all nations.

We have to ask ourselves to engineer these goals such that we can manage to live with 9 billion people sharing one planet.

In a great, human dignified way.

And the place best to start that- as in all other great achievement in our global civilization- *by the self.*

That's why you may be reading this book.

And that's why you may want to meet with us

I dare to say the following, and in general:

The present organizational forms and formats chosen, globally, regionally and locally –

And in our political and business community organizations- for the attainment of the UN Sustainable Development goals in our mainstream economics in our countries of the world – are not yet attuned and fit..

Won't make it.

We may expect to see a continued fight, flight and stride of established economic interests, social crisis and/or environmental recoveries- in and between nations and corporations.

The organizational forms and foundations we have chosen today- for the progression of the UN SDGs and our national economies- are simply not yet zippered enough[115], committed and attuned , made subtle and to the times we see ourselves in.

The fundamentals that have build our present economic and organizational believes, our companies, our civil societies, our politics, our international relationships still also needs transformation- before we are ready to achieve and deliver the UN Sustainable Developments for real.

We can't have this transformation, if we don't allow ourselves , and to first to see of what it is we are invited to re-consider, re-engineer and re-imagine.

So- the first step in the assurance of our Leadership Performances, of our lives, of our children and children lives is our responsibility and decision to make ourselves a Learner and a Leader.

Of a new kind.

---

[115] Zippered relations implies that the transformation organisation and programs runs from Top-to-Bottom and from Bottoms-up, connecting communities, with cities, with regions, with countries, with businesses, with regional blocks, with the global community. The Paris Climate Change agreement is an attempt to do so.

A Leader that dares to become a Pupil (=learner, listener) again, and understand that it needs to De-learn and Lead something new.

A Leader that understand that progressing today's is managing, but is not leading our new ways.

That is why I am so enthusiastic about Laudato Si!

That is why I am so enthusiastic about Assisi, Saint Francis and the Spirit of Assisi .

As they emulate the road and journeys we, as Leaders in Business and in Governments, may need and wish to take.

They help us to reflect and they help us to converse - allowing us to become truly an instrument of Peace and Progress,

Changing the way we see things.

Changing what we see and experience as important, and what constitutes success.

Building Peace , Building Human Dignity and Building Respect for Nature - in *all* programs and steps - as we go.

Conversion of an Oil Man - to A man of Energy, UN Sustainable Development, Peace and All Good.

When I stepped outside the walls of the Shell Group, a Major International Oil Company- now well over 5 years ago- and to start a small organisation in search for the new and better pathways for our beloved Energy Industry, I knew my life was to change, and that the changes could be profound.

My search for better pathways was inspired by the realisation, then and there- that our World was Changing and needed us (the OilCo's , the Corporates, The Energy Professional, the Energy Sector)- to change

And I realized that we needed to find the better bridges between Rich and Poor, East and West, North and South, the Conventional Energy Sector and the Renewable/ Innovation Energy sector- and in order to attain the dream we held true:

Energy- available, affordable, sustainable- to all.

Free of concerns.

Healing the Shadow Sides and Making room for the New

The path of Redemption and Service

When I stepped outside the walls of the Shell Group, - inside its walls we *knew* already actually quite a lot about the complexities and possible volatilities of the times to come, the capital markets and our corporations, the mis-alignments between what the market needs and what we deliver, and we *knew* already quite a bit between the strong-hold relations between Oil Price (High or Low), Energy and Finance and the impact this can have on local Economies (2008 Financial Crisis)

When I stepped outside the walls - we *knew* the key World Energy Scenario's to be expected, including considerations from the Club Of Rome and the rise in energy demands from a growing world population, including its' consuming wealth demands (resource scarcities, exploration creaming curves, the un-sustainability of unconventional resources), shifts and dynamics in Geo-politics -and we *knew* Climate Change, the loss of nature, air pollution from coal, gas and diesel, environmental concerns (e.g. unconventional, fracking, deep, sour, and arctic field developments) and the rapid rise of energy consuming demands, including the rise and shifts of new technologies.

When I stepped outside the walls - we *knew* that energy scarcity or volatile prices could give rise to tensions or new opportunity seeking in existing (energy-value chain) relationships, in economies (job creations or losses), or could give rise to the Geo-politics of emotions.

In essence- we *knew* already quite a lot about (some of) the realities in our beloved Energy Sector.

But as the journey of my consulting practice started, somewhere over 2012, I must admit- *what an enormous mountain of new lessons have I received*- ever since I left the protected walls of a Major International Oil Company.

I cannot describe this differently to you.

The learnings, the lessons, the insights feel today as we have seen, reached and climbed a (first) Mountain Top.

On our way.

As on this first Mountain Top- I have learned to see the possible and probable pathways that can help us to attain and better integrate Sustainable Energy, Sustainable Development and Sustainable Societies- inside and outside the present complexities of Geo-politics, the present elite, chosen organisations and tones of voices, capital markets and business ways of preserving working interests, and the present ways we are organized and behave- in our businesses, in finance and in our governments,.

As I have come to see in and with the Eyes of the Most Seniors in our beloved Energy Sector, and the ones who presently "own" or "play" in the energy value chains and sustainable development, as well those who are presently advocating or inspired to make the change

As I have come to see in the Eyes of the Young and the ones who are in most need.

And on this journey - step-by-step- I have also come to see and meet with the Good, the Bad and the Ugly.

The Ego in Man, the Status Quo, The Lobby, The Repeat of Leadership dogma's or re-jection to open-up, to innovate or to progress, and - at times- the Selfish character of nations, governments, people and organisations.

Of course, ever since year 2012- the face of the Energy Sector has seen profound changes.

Good ones.

Let us not forget the year 2015- with the adoption of the UN Sustainable Development Goals, Paris Climate Change Agreement and the break-through in commercial pricing of some of the renewables, business model re-inventions of utilities (e.g. the new E-on), energy efficiency around our industries and homes or new mobility inventions (e.g. autonomous electric mobility) has done or will be doing.

But let us also not *fool* ourselves with some of these *tokens* and *small coins thrown "at it"* (by the present incumbents in the resource holding nations and energy corporations) - as the latest annual statistic review and energy outlook 2017 from BP again so clearly and vividly depicts .

(or some of the better journalists have revealed over these years- in one-to-one interviews with staff from these larger energy corporations)

I suggest you re-read my more sober observations on this matter.

Go to observations

Through all the *"smoke and mirrors"*, and the - at times- rather ill-advised *"policy instruments"* assumed by Governments, and advised by the present in incumbents of the energy corporations *(the ones that truly know)* - and their highly paid management consultants -and which are subsequently taken on-board "as almost the holy grail and truth" by some of our nations and global institutes such as UNFCCC, IMF/World Bank, IEA and so on:

I can just simply observe and say;

We haven't yet truly and honestly understood or started with Energy and Energy transition inside the walls of our better corporations

We haven't yet truly and honestly understood or started with Energy and Energy Transition inside the walls of the administrations of some our better resource holding energy nations.

We haven't yet truly and honestly started with transition of our economies and societies in order to attain sustainable living and working conditions- to all.

We are still very much in a Econo-Me-game, an Energy-to- Finance game, and not yet in a We-game or a Social Sustainable Pathway Game to All.

(and of course we are not to be naïve- and we know first-hand the many practical or so called realistic reasons why certain things cannot move that fast, or can't move at all- but that is not the point)

We are yet *far away* and removed from an *open and honest* approach to make our energy sector *truly* better.[116]

And that hurts.

As time - in this case- matters.

It matters for a better Energy Balance in our world. It matters for the Paris Climate Change Agreement. It matters to the attainment of the UN Sustainable Development Goals.

The last AGM's of our Western Oil Companies gave "crystal clear voice" how our present fortresses of wealth are being protected.

Clearly visible to all to see. Willingly and perhaps- a little bit - unwillingly.

---

[116] e.g. also read the more recent opinion of President Duterte of Phillipines on this issue (July 2016).

But let us also not spare the ones who advocate for change, the environmental lobbyists or the ones who press and want to imprint their own views and interests:

How different are you really from the present incumbents: in form and in mind?

Today- my practice *has learned a little more* on Global Change, Energy Architecture Development , Sustainable Development- and our "new global sustainability movement and elites' that presently reign..

and

Today- my practice *learned a little more* on how our present societies, our corporations and our governments- in the East and in the West, in the North and in the South, including the UN organisations and agencies, acts, behaves and works on these invitations and calls for *better* change - on the aggregate- as we can clearly see on our horizons.

How politicized we, at times, are- and how important our faces and our words have become in front of a camera.

But one thing we can (all) observe:

What we think, what we say and what we do- is often *not congruent* (and I say this here quite politely).

"Resistance to change"- or lobbies for self-interests ever so much visible or a little bit more hidden from the public face.

In our Nations, in Our Corporations, by our Business Entrepreneurs and in our International Trade relations, and so much more.

And every day we learn a little more on this: *as such we may feel ourselves true pupils for life.*

Of course -part of the answer lies - in our abilities to unlock New Visions (and Workable Transition Strategies to attain e.g. UN Sustainable development Goals) - on locations, in the regions- as well in and between our international partnerships,:

To heal what is broken, to fix our shadow sides and to re-imagine a better, and better balanced energy-economy future.

Strategies that no longer are only good for the self (*opportunistic or window-dressing*), but are also *truly* there to serve and support the healing and improvement of our present and past, our humanity and nature on location, including preservation of mother Earth.

Locally, Regionally and internationally.

In the East and in the West. In the North and in the South.

and

(One of) the other elements ("in our winning mix") is of course *our chosen organisational forms* and our style and tone of voice in or Leadership over these Transformations and Changes - helping to attain and integrate our Energy Sector Agenda with that of the Sustainable Development Goals.

To heal , to fix and to re-imagine the ways we lead , finance and organize ourselves

But let us not be naïve:

The present world order and the aggregate of our Human Civilisation truly *asks, begs, and invites* us to become congruent.

To become "whole".

Inside our Nations, inside our Corporations, and inside Ourselves.

Today - we are not.

The present world order and contexts we see ourselves placed in- with all its' rivalries and demands for competitions- the power, the money and the corrupted- *above* and *under* the table, *hidden* and *in the open*- makes it *ever so complex* and difficult to us *to become* and live our lives congruent.

And that is sad.

As it *in this* that we can attain the true richness in our life and a true and honest meaning in ourselves, our corporations and our nations.

The right people doing the right things for the right reasons and heart intents.

Today we mix Fear with Hope.

Today we mix "Market Domination, Market Share, Shareholder Dividends, Needs of Being in Control" with "Allowing a More Beautiful World to Rise".

Today, we fear for losing *our* jobs, *our* security, *our* wealth, *our* life and life-styles, *our* little preserved paradises, *our* money, *our* self-interests

Fear for the others. *Fear* for unwanted changes. *Fear* of losing wealth or face. *Fear* of making mistakes, *Fear* of not having enough. *Fear* for missing on an opportunity. *Fear* for not reaching our financial goals or targets...

And as such- and with *this Fear*- we fail to truly allow and unlock the more Beautiful World- in and between us- that we know:

If you need some evidence in seeing this with your own eyes- I suggest you read this more sober news[117]:

If you like to understand of what further changes are required to heal, fix and re-image some of what is today the norm in the energy sector, I suggest you may find time to read the books The Prize, by Daniel Yergin, and Energy Autonomy: The Economic, Social and Technological Case for Renewable Energy, by Herman Scheer, who was the architect of the solar economy in Germany with the feed-in tariff and who is a proponent of moving to renewable energy.

The Prize tells the story of the DNA of the present oil and gas sector: the power games, the interests, the corruption, and the geopolitical energy security and economic rivalries.

This "energy games of thrones" is still very much in place.

Energy Autonomy contains Herman Scheer's proposal and plan to make energy available, affordable and sustainable to all. We have yet to see the better dialogue(s) in order to keep this dream alive.

---

[117] War costs us $13.6 trillion. So why do we spend so little on peace? https://t.co/whKvo6BiBT via @wef #war #peace

— H-Christian Preymann (@HCPreymann) June 14, 2016

Conversion of Happiness.

It is really wonderful.

To be Happy.

Happy with what is. Happy what you are occupied with. Happy with your friends and family.

Happy days. Happy times.

Youngsters, generally speaking, have a "good knack and feel for this".

People, when they grow a little older, at times, start to carry some weight and stature (responsibilities) or become a little *cynical* on *how* life is, and what to expect or what this is to bring to thee.

They become un-happy. Or they feel they can no longer be truly happy. They "lost touch" with their Youth, Enthusiasm and the more true Passions of Life.

In parts of the West, as well in the rest of our global village, a new movement and wave is taking root, and based on some Buddhist understandings:

Happiness is a Choice.

I agree.

But may I observe here also that the form of choice made by some of these present *self-elected happiness- converts* is not mine.

I have opted to choose and walk a somewhat different road of happiness.

Let me briefly explain:

Latest health reports on the effects of today's information [118]overload paints us a solemn picture of an ever more becoming dependent consuming audience (addicted) to a multi-tasking and streams of (passive aggressive) information, with ever less time allowed for deepening and more creative and life-meaning thoughts, actions or attunement with the direct visible and invisible- human , divine, serene and natural environment.

This is true in the private free environment, as this phenomena can also been seen and witnessed in the corporate and institutionalized organisations.

---

[118] E.g. Guardian article, etc.

It was Pope Francis- and his visit and address to the Board of the World Food Organization in June 2016, stated:

We live in an interconnected world marked by instant communications. Geographical distances seem to be shrinking. We can immediately know what is happening on the other side of the planet. Communications technologies, by bringing us face to face with so many tragic situations, can help, and have helped, to mobilize responses of compassion and solidarity. Paradoxically though, this apparent closeness created by the information highway seems daily to be breaking down. An information overload is gradually leading to the "naturalization" – pardon the neologism – of extreme poverty. In other words, little by little we are growing immune to other people's tragedies, seeing them as something "natural". We are bombarded by so many images that we see pain, but do not touch it; we hear weeping, but do not comfort it; we see thirst but do not satisfy it. All those human lives turn into one more news story. While the headlines may change, the pain, the hunger and the thirst remain; they do not go away.
===

We need to "de-naturalize" extreme poverty, to stop seeing it as a statistic rather than a reality. Why? Because poverty has a face! It has the face of a child; it has the face of a family; it has the face of people, young and old. It has the face of widespread unemployment and lack of opportunity. It has the face of forced migrations, and of empty or destroyed homes.
We cannot "naturalize" the fact that so many people are starving. We cannot simply say that their situation is the result of blind fate and that nothing can be done about it. Once poverty no longer has a face, we can yield to the temptation of discussing "hunger", "food" and "violence" as concepts, without reference to the real people knocking on our doors today. Without faces and stories, human lives become statistics and we run the risk of bureaucratizing the sufferings of others. Bureaucracies shuffle papers; compassion – not pity, but com-passion, suffering with – deals with people.
Here I believe that we have much to do. In addition to everything already being done, we need to work at "denaturalizing" and "debureaucratizing" the poverty and hunger of our brothers and sisters. This requires us to intervene on different scales and levels, focusing on real people who are suffering and starving, while drawing upon an abundance of enthusiasm and potential that we need to help exploit.

Let me add a small and perhaps relevant observation – from my hand.

I happen to believe that when we consume "suffering and suffering images and stories from around the world, and at our fingertips in our offices or in our homes"- I have come to see and believe that by this act, we are indirectly inflicted and connected.

Our happiness can no longer exist, in trueness, if we are or have become aware of suffering elsewhere, and "choose to look the other way" or "have become indifferent"- *in our hearts and minds*.

Our happiness can no longer exist, in reality, if we see and have made ourselves connected with the sufferings we observed, first hand.

Our life, and our life meaning becomes one of compassion and care, when we dare to see that our true joy, happiness *and* freedom is connected with our abilities to grow and nurture our "human heart and soul" - between each other[119]- and especially to those that vulnerable and need our care.

To live our lives full, and to do what is possible and what is asked for[120] in our lives and in our ways- helping and giving for the other.

Add to this another solemn observation and realization, and one that is often used also in combination with the Paris Climate Change agreement- , is:

Some of the sufferings elsewhere, are based upon some of our consuming habits, free and happy life habits, here.

This can be quite confronting.

How would you feel if you knew that a storm and flood in Bangladesh, and that has killed thousands and thousands of poor people and citizens- may actually have been caused by your joy of driving, transporting and consuming happily?

How do you think the son or daughter feels in Bangladesh, that become to believe or realize that the storm or flood that took away her father or mother may have been caused by western (or eastern e.g. Chinese) decadence?

How do you feel if you know that the coal, oil and/or gas that fuels your tank or powers your home- has been made by labourers who were suffering from unhealthy work practices, and have been produced in a natural environment without too much concern for its' impact or longer-term implications?

How do you feel in your 5-star hotel room, when you know that the breakfast that was being served, or the hotel room that has been cleaned was made up and done by a boy or girl that had to travel at 3 am in the morning by foot and cycle, and to arrive in time in the hotel, to serve you?

How would you feel that his or her wages in a week or month is less than what you pay today for the room, or earn in wages by the hour?

How do you feel if the clothes you wear or the rooms you occupy have been made by people who suffer from lack of care and income?

The complexities and intimacies of our today's global village asks and invites us to reflect again of what it is *what makes meaning in our life and country*, and what it is what comprise and constitutes a happy, meaningful and responsible , sustainable living life.

---

[119] In religious/spiritual circles: also in communion with the Divine

[120] In religious/spiritual circles one often describe this process: receiving ones call or calling.

New awareness asks and begs us to reach for new frontiers, new relationships[121] and new dimensions in our human development and in our happiness.

Was it 1000's of years ago- that we could live and thrive in our own tribe, away from the other.

Was it till this century that we could live and thrive happy in our own city, national boundaries and towns.

Today- our interdependent and inter-connected world asks and invites us to become "whole".

To become truly free, responsible and caring.

This asks for a new form of leadership (stewardship) and "a new form of tone of voice" - in and between ourselves, in relations to the other, and as part of the whole.

That's why I like so much the UN Sustainable development goals.

That's why I like so much the words and meanings of Pope Francis and in his Laudato Si!

Our happiness becomes connected with *our* calling, and our happiness become connected with *our wholeness*: being truly free and committed on our ways.

With the sharing of some of these *Tales of Conversion*, I invite you to reflect on these elements in your lives, and hope to see some you with some new consciousness and joy on your pathway.

I *am* most happy on this way.

---

[121] Between the Rich and the Poor

Noblesse Oblige

It's rather easy for me to write these lines.

As I truly believe this.

I am not born in-wealth[122], but I may have been born with some special talents and gifts.

It are these talents and gifts, that I today employ and share with you- as my token of good will.

It's my Noblesse Oblige.[123]

The same may today hold true and be valid for Countries and Corporations.

Countries and Corporations may see that they have some *special* skills, capabilities, wealth or talents- that other countries and societies would grossly benefit from.

It is a further insight and awareness that these gifts may not be best served to profiteer from, or to take advantages, dominion and possessions- over others.

They are there, given and bestowed, as a blessing of our good fortunes and the results of some of our collective hard work- over time.

Now- let's do some brief history.

And very much simplified.

And let's look at some of the most recent developments in our wealth and wealth distribution:

BERKELEY – The Berkeley economist Barry Eichengreen recently gave a talk in Lisbon about inequality that demonstrated one of the virtues of being a scholar of economic history. Eichengreen, like me, glories in the complexities of every situation, avoiding oversimplification in the pursuit of conceptual clarity. This disposition stays the impulse to try to explain more about the world than we can possibly know with one simple model.

For his part, with respect to inequality, Eichengreen has identified six first-order processes at work over the past 250 years.

---

[122] Though not unwealthy, and as I have enjoyed quite a wealthy life and lifestyles, before the call for my practice works took me to today.
[123] https://en.wikipedia.org/wiki/Noblesse_oblige

The first is the widening of Britain's income distribution between 1750 and 1850, as the gains from the British Industrial Revolution went to the urban and rural middle class, but not to the urban and rural poor.

Second, between 1750 and 1975, income distribution also widened globally, as some parts of the world realized gains from industrial and post-industrial technologies, while others did not. For example, in 1800, American purchasing power parity was twice that of China; by 1975 it was 30 times that of China.

The third process is what is known as the First Age of Globalization, between 1850 and 1914, when living standards and labor productivity levels converged in the global north. During this time, 50 million people left an overcrowded agricultural Europe for resource-rich new settlements. They brought their institutions, technologies, and capital with them, and the wage differential between Europe and these new economies shrank from roughly 100% to 25%.

This mostly coincided with the Gilded Age between 1870 and 1914, when domestic inequality rose in the global north as entrepreneurship, industrialization, and financial manipulation channeled new gains mostly to the wealthiest families.

Gilded Age inequality was significantly reversed during the period of social democracy in the global north, between 1930 and 1980, when higher taxes on the wealthy helped pay for new government benefits and programs. But the subsequent and last stage brings us to the current moment, when economic policy choices have again resulted in a widening of the distribution of gains in the global north, ushering in a new Gilded Age.

Making a long story short, we can state that the industrial revolution in England-has been (one of the main) success stories and sources for the on-set of transportation, industrialisation and work globalisation we experience ourselves in today.

In these early days of industrialisation, England's technological, military and administrative (governance) advantage led herself to reign over more than 100 colonies abroad.

It had become a Super-Power.

Almighty by its' fierce military and shipping, it's industrial technologies (steam-egines and beyond) .

Now, turn the clock 200 years forwards- and we see a complete different picture.

England has been overtaken by US and China in its' industrial and political prowess.

The colonies have all been made independent, following the aftermath of World War II, and our sentiments and ideas over this colonial period [124] are mixed at best.

Following the independence of all these colonies (including those of Spain, Portugal, France, Belgium, Italy, Netherlands, etc.) – a new period of development aid took shape and hold, in our global village and international relationships.

Foreign Aid.

As part of the United Nations, Governments agreed some new "tasks and targets" in foreign aid and development aid to the former colonies, and the least developed nations: making-up a new force of good.

A whole wide range of help (or Foreign Aid) agencies, not-for-profits blossomed in the West, and were created as bridge-heads and functions to channel this foreign aid funds in their applications overseas.

During Rio, Rio plus 20, and the subsequent negotiations for the Paris Climate Change agreement and the UN Sustainable development programs, a new atmosphere and vision has been taking shape.

Foreign aid is to be replaced with a new form of payment and international trade relations based on fair and equitable business principles and a combination of capability, technology transfer, and finance.

And that may be some very good news, as the donor and adoption countries can no longer *see or feel* themselves in a parent-child relationship, and better see some new opportunities and better trade conditions with countries as wide and diverse as China- G77/G130 and seek for new equality in trade, without further conditions on human rights or development conditions.

But let us not forget something:

The history, pain, wounds and suffering, at times put on people, communities and nations, by the lack of or rather submissively led progress is not without its present day emotions or consequences.

Let us also not forget that in many of these former colonial countries around, it is still not easy to see a stable government, administrative or industrial performing culture.

Today, we can see ODA/ and foreign aid re-branded, and today, we can see governments abound making it part of the Paris Climate Change Agreement and the UN Sustainable development goals.

---

[124] (the good, the bad and the ugly)

I have seen in the eyes of the man and woman in our (western nations= ministries[125] , and who are to organise and dispense these funds overseas.

I have seen in their eyes some fear that we may be entering a phase of a new Pandora's box and endless "black hole" – financial games, and where ever year – new and more calls are being placed on State Public finance for loss and compensation (liabilities) , adaptation, resilience and new capacity building. [126]

Innovation and improvement of the social and local country fabric takes time.

And it takes good caring expertise.

Somehow, and some way, our foreign aid and development work over the last couple of 50 years has done lots' of good, but is and has also be part and member of being not good enough or "not good enough at all".

It had a shadow-side[127] connected to it. And it proofed emotionally laden.

In too many instances, and I am sure, our national corporations and elite have taken some good advantages of seeing themselves in - "quite special[128]" - good business and country deals overseas, without too many responsibilities tied to these deals to care for a whole and integrated human development.[129]

Sure- thousands and thousands of hospitals, schools, universities and townships have been built.

But somewhere, and along the line, we may have forgotten what it is, and what it takes to get the best from us, and the best from them- aligned and attuned- such that some more sustainable, lasting and true miracles can and could be done.

It has to do with "our soul and with our heart".

It has to do with our deeper commitment to truly help and serve each other, forego selfish-ness or priorities only for ourselves-. To forego our ways.

I will not deny, nor defy – the many missionary and exemplary country development works that have been done by my predecessors from my continent and nations.

Nevertheless all that, and again first hand witnessed, I have seen some of the arrogances in our leaderships and diplomatic relationship buildings, some

---

[125] North-West Europe
[126] E.g. President Duerte of the Phillipines, July 2016
[127] E.g. State and Business Corruptions, Self-interests. Using Foreign Aid to advance export of National Goods and services
[128] E.g. American Exceptionalism. Former British and French Colonial Empire Arrogances.
[129] A fact that China is improving upon, and the Countries are now actively advocating and lobbying for.,

demonstrations of discriminations, judgements (on culture and poverties) and so on.

"Max Havelaar"[130] is a famous book in the Netherlands, and written in the times of the Dutch colonial past in Indonesia.

I quote here from Wikipedia:

> **Max Havelaar: Or the Coffee Auctions of the Dutch Trading Company** (Dutch: *Max Havelaar, of de koffi-veilingen der Nederlandsche Handel-Maatschappy*) *is an 1860 novel by* Multatuli *(the* pen name *of Eduard Douwes Dekker), which played a key role in shaping and modifying* Dutch colonial policy *in the* Dutch East Indies *in the nineteenth and early twentieth century. In the novel, the protagonist, Max Havelaar, tries to battle against a corrupt government system in* Java, *which was then a Dutch* colony.
>
> ...
>
> *In the novel, the story of Max Havelaar, a Dutch colonial administrator, is told by two diametrically opposed characters: the hypocritical coffee merchant Droogstoppel, who intends to use Havelaar's manuscripts to write about the coffee trade, and the romantic German apprentice Stern, who takes over when Droogstoppel loses interest in the story. The opening chapter of the book nicely sets the tone of the* satirical *nature of what is to follow, with Droogstoppel articulating his pompous and mercenary world-view at length. At the very end of the novel Multatuli himself takes the pen and the book culminates in a vocal denunciation of Dutch colonial policies and a plea to the king of the Netherlands to intervene on behalf of his Indonesian subjects*

Let me share you a small observation for our better tomorrows.

Whilst times may have been a little different: The Spirit of "Max Havelaar" is still very much around us today- and both in the host governments as well in those of the overseas countries abroad,-[131] - as well in the mercantile boardrooms and of our governments and companies in the East[132] as in the West,.

Over the last decades, I have witnessed first-hand, the experiences and ways of going about things in our beloved Oil and Gas sector.

---

[130] https://en.wikipedia.org/wiki/Max_Havelaar

[131] (re. e.g. India and China)
[132] Only very recently, and in July 2016, we could read in our news the sad fact of the 10,000 Indian workers being laid off in Saudi Arabia without any money, food or living means . This is and is becoming again rather typical.

The History of Oil and their Multinational Oil companies, has also been the history of us telling the other (the host country) how things need to be managed, and what profits to take home.[133]

Whilst today, we can see many improvements in the ways the Western Multi-national companies operate in this respect, but you may fear with me.- how this process is still being done in other energy, infrastructure, manufacturing and producing companies and governments of our globe village around.

And it's not only minerals or commodities. "Max Havelaar" is actually still very much present in *all* of our overseas companies and government -trades., again from the East and the West.

---

[133] E.g. in books like: The Prize, The 7 Sisters , 100 years Shell, etc.

From Leadership to Stewardship

Leaders and Leadership today is a challenging experience.

Let's agree: our world today is not yet ideal – nor perfect.

At times – we are just faced or overwhelmed with complexities and conflicting and opposing demands, that it becomes almost sheer impossible to manage and lead all these well.

To prioritize and order.

As we move "beyond the glass ceiling into the corner office" all our acts, moves and decisions are seen and observed – not only by the own team, the company, the government administration- but also by the stakeholders, the media and more and more in the eye of public and opinion.

Leadership today, and if we want to do this in style- is to "live and breath" in the open.

To be transparent.

To be whole.

The "alignment" between the needs of society, the organization, the role and our self – is essential in order to perform best.

The temptation to grow own ego, our masks and brand or self-belief (in intuition, being right) – not in the least fuelled by an inner circle of supporters, can be detrimental.

To that end, and organizational dynamics has proven this time and time again- leadership today is an art.

As much as leadership is about the abilities to manage large and complex societies and organisations, it's also a path of inner wisdom and personal growth.[1]

To be able to look with rather "mild and wise" eyes to the situation we are in.

Not all leaders have had the chance to mature themselves in this way- before they have worked themselves in a position of power or influence.

Modern day leadership asks and invites us to combine a couple of talents and characteristics:

To be compassionate and warm in our hearts and in our relationships, creating the optimal holding space for the team and more complex social constellations to perform, as well as being able to overlook and help to guide the direction, the performances and deliveries- at times – as an army general overlooking the battle field- when times are tough- or asks for change.

So- this "hard and soft" in leadership- call it "situational leadership"- is an essence of being able to stand the test of times, and being able to drive the transformation forwards.

Leadership without a moral or ethical compass are rudderless.

Leadership that aims to leads transformational processes, needs to transform (change) themselves first.

The famous saying and statement by Gandhi may proof right:

> "You must be the change you want to see in the world."

Leadership with a vision and mission on making human development, our lives, times and our ways truly better deserve our support and attention.

It's quite subtle and needs leaders who can work fully and wholly with "heart, mind and soul" in this process.

Add to that the complexities, the tempo and dynamics of our societies today, and especially also the complexities in the more "hard-nosed and competing and rivaling" political, business, economic and banking arena's and sectors of our societies- and you understand that we are looking at some very special abilities and skills.

To train, nurture and reflect on "our state of being" when in leadership becomes hence an essential element for success.

Managing self

Our journey into leadership may start with the self. By making a start (or an attempt) to understand the self better, our conscious and unconscious patterns of thoughts and behaviors, we may rise to the challenge of becoming a little bit more aware of our own perspectives- an thus of others.

Interesting research has been done by the Mayo Clinic team in the US. A team of psychologists, doctors, therapists are working here to better understand the difference between happy people and the not so happy people.

The results of their (scientific) findings has been the source of the book written by Dan Baker: "What happy people know". The basic difference between happy and not-so-happy people is in the functioning and ways of the brain and thought processes: either thinking (and thus speaking and acting) out of compassion (love) or of a higher brain response or from a more reptilian brain (fear).

You can't mix or fix those two themes in one brain, and the good news further is that we can train our minds (and beings) to become much more compassionate:

creating positive acts. Another form by which this message is given to people, and potential leaders, is by spiritual leaders such as e.g. the Dalai Lama.

Finally- today's neuroscientists seem to agree that regular prayer or meditation (or attentive focus) can help to grow more awareness and awakening of ourselves.

To grow our capacity for compassion and understanding. To grow our conscious mind more into unconscious area of our mind. To be more at peace and ease with whatever is.

To better understand and see the Ego- The self. For a professional, who wants to excel in Leadership in her or his profession- the invitation is to find the own ways of nurturing and doing this. This can be through sport, culture, family, nature, through religion, spirituality or other means – as long as this inner source of energy, wisdom and content is being nurtured and kept whole..

Why is this of such an importance?

Whenever we are confronted or expose ourselves to dynamic environments, with large uncertainties and change- this strong inner-self, our connection and communion with source, will be the source of balance within.

Especially in the last lonely mile (every transformation project or business seems to have a period of crisis where the leader is thrown on his or her self), at headwinds or when the going gets tough..

Managing others and change

Ever since the great construction works of the past, human mankind has found and defined organizational forms by which great achievements could be made. Mobilizing 1000's and 1000's of people, materials and goods – and in accordance with a plan (or blueprint) for the realization of something big.

In order to achieve these great projects (or wars- the military is another great example of learning how to master an army in extreme (uncertain) situations), men created organizational hierarchy and functions (roles) by which individuals had to work and abide by.

For periods when there was time, but also for situations when there was duress or stress.

Our modern day corporate and governmental organizations much resemble this core principle. A hierarchical form by which there is a leadership for (urgent and important or strategic) decision making at the Top, and Executive (or operational layers) for realization.

Next to that- each and every organization has its' own culture or DNA. In each (professional) organization, people are hired in to do or execute roles. Dis-harmony (or trouble) rises when either the organization, role or person hired for that role s not are aligned.

That's when we see trouble in real life.

In our government administrative bodies, in our corporate boardrooms, but also in project or business units. The whole is not any longer attuned or in flow. There is friction.

To have an eye for the constitution and constellation of the tri-pod: *organization, role and person* is a leadership role.

To understand whatever in the organization, or whomever needs adjustment in order to restore harmony or health in an organisation.

Sometimes the organization needs healing from fear (re. what happy people know), sometimes the role needs to be redefined (as it does not jive well with the aspired culture). This is especially true for roles and positions of innovation and transformational change. Those roles can easily attract allergic reactions in organizations.

Now comes a paradox:

A great (government and business) leader may combine the best leadership styles from a) the Military (or e.g. great project works) as well from b) our Wisdom leaders (e.g. Pope Francis) as well from c) the Entrepreneurial or Innovator Spirited (e.g. Gates, Jobs, Musk, Ford, Edison, Rockefeller) as well d) between the Feminine and Masculine

Military leaders know as no other that they can only move as fast, and as agile as their people allow them to do: in order to get the results. Military leadership is further focussed , second to none, on the understanding of the external and internal landscape and situation of their campaigns..("situational analysis/ getting the results as no other")

Wisdom leaders know what is best for the group, and over time, see-ing the situation from many different perspectives[134], and working from compassion for humanity (the others and self) - in Spirit and at Heart.[135]

Entrepreneurs and New Frontier Scientists have the minds of imagination, of creativity, the life force of change and innovation- and can be truly creative and "Free in Mind".

Leading today, without our ability to blend the best of what Female can bring us (compassion, heart, care) with that of the more Masculine force- and what I have seen and witnessed, is leading ourselves today hopelessly astray.

A great leader, to my mind, and for what I have seen and witnessed, combines them *all*- either in person or in his or her (inner-circle , organization) team.

---

[134] Including divine and spirit

[135] The Dalai Lama once joked: I am happy that I am not a business leader as my company would be broke within a year. I am too compassionate for people.

That may be one of the great paradoxes of (situational) leadership.

In Leadership- there are also nuances and styles. A creative not-for-profit company will have another DNA as a large and bureaucratic government agency and as such will require a different character of leadership (role expectation) for its transformational roadmaps, goals and plans.

Another aspect what makes a difference in suitable leadership is:

Size.

Size matters.

Small can be more beautiful.

An organization can retain and remain informal ("family-feel") if we know-how to keep the headcount below 50.

Above 50, and as experience so far has indicated so far, an organization seems to need to formalize its' workforce into procedures and processes.

Research into the styles of corporate leadership in the US has been done by Jim Collins in his book: Good to Great.

In his book, published in 2001, Collins makes the point for so-called level 5 leadership styles. A leader which is beyond the need to position him or her self in the center of attention and power-making: the otherwise so well-know charisma leaders.

In his research, Jim found evidence that leadership based on the organization and team had a better chance of becoming great. His tripod for greatness existed on three principles: 1. What you are deeply passionate about 2. What you can be the best in the world 3. What drives your economic engine.

Spencer Stuart's Thomas Neff and James Citrin "Lessons from the Top", a book looking at the top 100 CEO in US Fortune-500, released also in 2001 – actually found a somewhat different nuance in differentiating good from great, and this may make the point on our journey into leadership – we are all students for life..

A perhaps much simpler way to look at leadership style (or to learn to practice this) is by adopting Servant Leadership. The whole idea behind this leadership practice (over others) is to think, act and work from the intent to let others (and the organization) blossom,

Not yourself- but the other.

To act as a coach or steward over the healthy growth of others.

Truly turning leadership 180 degrees around.

By this simple act of deeper Leadership Conversion- everything changes:

Our views on Life and Leadership, Our Governance, Governance models, Organizational forms and principles, relationships, business principles, etc. etc.- this all becomes a little different.

This process of a more deeper leadership and organizational form conversion is – to my mind- very much relevant, if not a priority- for the attainment of our program objectives:

The attainment of the Paris Climate Change agreement and UN Sustainable Development.

Making the rise of an integral human and sustainable development core and priority in all our programs, decisions and our ways.

The good news is:

This call for Leadership Conversion has been on-going now for at least 40 years in the richer OECD countries, and can be seen and experienced in different stages of maturity, evolution, shapes and forms.[136]

Our call to see us in Assisi not one of the least.

As our call, may support you to change the way you see things.

Changing what you see and experience as important, and what constitutes your success.

Building Peace , Building Human Dignity and Building Respect for Nature - in *all* programs and steps - as you go.

---

[136] Servant Leadership, Conscious Capitalism, Business Spirituality, Heart for Business, Business Ethics, Sociocracy , Intentional Communities/Eco-villages, etc. etc.

Chapter 3: Preparing for Change

Walking on the path of Sustainable Development and Paris Climate Change Agreement

The Global UN Sustainable Development Goals from Energy for One World

I will use this paragraph to share some of my reflections on "What it may take (to the World) to transit from the Millennium Development Goals to the Sustainable Development Goals.

I base this dialogue on the open conversation I participated in – during the 2015 ECOSOC platform conversation and theme:

"Managing the transition from the Millennium Development Goals to the sustainable development goals: What it will take"

And of course – I will be a little specific- when I speak on issues of Energy & Sustainability- but most of my observations may also be quite handy and applicable for the other themes and goals (17) in the proposed program.

First of all- I would like to share – that I am excited. Excited by this UN program, and excited by the opportunities , the new hopes and new realizations this program may actually unleash.

As the program touches "a new order of human enlightenment" in it's program orientation goals

Let's build the World We Want.

Let's build sustainable societies for all

How are we going to live together- as 9 billion people- sharing one planet?

I look at the program of Sustainable Development – as a new pact, a new opportunity- between the nations, the governments, companies (business community), academia and society.

In the East and in the West, The North and in the South.

I look at this program with new hopes and dreams for the poor and deprived, the working middle-class *and* the elites of this world.

As this program- when done well – can actually unleash the best in us. It can shine and bring new radiance in ourselves and in our societies. A new radiance of caring and sharing. Of shared stewardship. Of hope. Of can do.

The program- and when done well- can and may help to change or transform today's gridlock and sometimes competitive trenches in the geopolitical arena, and may empower and nurture the more hopeful and healthy dialogues and mind-sets between ourselves:

Of collaboration. Of crossing borders and cultures. Of listening and caring. Of giving and sharing. Of diversity and inclusiveness.

Yes- Let's unlock the best in humanity. Let's improve the ways we are going to relate, and let's resolve some of the most urgent and pressing issues facing mankind (or of our living together).

As such- I and my practice is full-heartingly in.

Let's look at the individual section queries at this 2015 ECOSOC dialogue– and let me share with you, some first and very brief observation on our opportunities therein:-

Policy choices and mindset change for an integrated agenda

What are current examples of an integrated approach to policy-making and what is their degree of success? What are the existing tools and approaches for operationalizing an integrated approach at different levels?

What are the approaches to, and changes in behaviour required for integrated policy-making for the new agenda? What kind of communication strategies are needed for changing this mindset?

What are the potential complementarities and synergies involved in the pursuit of a universal agenda at the national, regional and global levels?

Required adaptation by institutions, structures and individuals

What types of changes and adaptation in institutions and structures will be needed at the national, regional and global levels to facilitate a smooth transition to a post-2015 era? What are the necessary corresponding changes in the roles and responsibilities of all partners?

To what extent are existing global institutions and policy frameworks ready to adopt and implement a more integrated approach to development? What adjustments may be needed to ensure that governments, the UN system and other partners respond to the universal and unified agenda and deliver equitable results for everyone?

What are the institutional and individual capacities required to facilitate a smooth transition from the MDGs to the SDGs?

Brief Observation(s):-

My practice works from the belief and understanding that our organizational forms determine to a large degree also our abilities to execute and deliver on our vision and strategies.

"*Function follows our Form*".

As we are transiting from the MDG towards the SDG- and we acknowledge that we are shape-shifting from an agenda solely focused on the "bottom of the pyramid" towards an agenda focused on the "whole of the pyramid"- it is clear that we may have to change our organizational agenda and form (of function deliveries) as well.

As the order and magnitude of the program is so much "bigger and all encompassing"- we may want to spend a little time in re-thinking of how we approach this massive new change challenge- as it will require new working pacts between and in businesses, governments, academia, and society.

Globally, regionally and locally.

And these working approaches and organisational forms may be different in the East and in the West, in the North and in the South.

Surely- this work has been done- in the many working groups preparing for the goals and the agenda- but as with everything- the conversion from vision/strategy to reality and realisation- in and over time- does need a little creativity and imagination- beyond the machinations of bureaucracy and our todays' working styles.

Earlier I have given a brief and presentation- on what may be needed in the field of Energy & Sustainability. At UN Level, and at the national and energy corporations level.

If of interest- I encourage you to read my briefing papers- Go to UN SDSN briefing papers– or to contact me in person.

For this note, and this conversation- I will stay a little generic.

The transition from MDG to SDG's – actually asks and invites us to Re-write, Re-form and Trans-form some of the existing beliefs, rules and experiences.

As we have the opportunity to make "room for the new"- to better listen to understand- we also can iron-out some of the inequalities in power, inequalities in communication and understandings, some of our sources of conflict, some of our unhealthy and unsustainable practices in our present industrial system.

Firstly- I would like to share a little video -presentation from Prof. Kotter.

Go to YouTube video

I think – and in this video-cast, he gives a good insight of what kind of new organisational dynamics we may want to aspire and organize in order to attain "living organisations" – who can adapt and transform to what we need.

This video-cast is applicable to individual corporations, but also is valid and applicable for administrations (UN, government) as well for the work between business, government, academia and the people!!

On the issue of Capacity and Capability building- on achieving the 17 goals- I would say and share the following, and based on my years in large-scale program and project portfolio management within the Shell Group:

The magic happens when the "vision and story" is compelling- and binds and passionates people, *all* people and member nations, to contribute and deliver.

The magic happens when the self-interests can be part and integrated in the whole.

The magic happens when we know-how to combine our vision with a workable strategy, manageable execution (delivery) operation and a (human) organization that ticks.

The magic happens when we keep trusting, keep deeply respecting the human dignities, the cultural nuances and the differences in perspectives we may have.

The magic happens when we are able to stay out of trouble, and collect and celebrate our early wins.

The magic happens when we keep loving what we are doing and keep serving the higher goals.

Now- surely- and in our modern days and ways- I know also the following:

Discipline and Fun in our Organization and our Deliveries are not each other enemy:

In other words: in order to realize and walk the path from vision, strategy to realization- we need good, compassionate and disciplined program management.

The kind of (executive) program management- business and industry is used to do.

Managing and monitoring such an extensive portfolio and integrated program- requires also perhaps some new management system(s) – beyond today's experiences within the UN.

To that end- I would like to propose a new, open and shared integrated management (governance) system, between government, business, academia and society- and which enables member countries and regions (e.g. Africa Union, EU, India, etc.) to self-assess, plan and share their organizational abilities to deliver and perform.

To conclude:

We have an extra-ordinary opportunity to do well. To raise the aspirations, to bring new hopes and help our human civilisation to a next realm of realization (maturity).

Our choice is if we are willing and able to open-up, to build and cross the various bridges, to integrate the UN Sustainable Development Goals into our mainstream business and trade relations, and to be creative and imaginative on the roads ahead:

To be able to organize ourselves for success: globally, regionally and locally.

That choice was rather simple for me and my practice to make.

I wish that same choice to all people, organizations and nations.

Integral Human and Sustainable Development : Connecting some dots

Over the last couple of years, I have made numerous training-workshop conversations- and presentations to the Executive Energy Professionals[137] on the issue of Global Change, Energy, Sustainable Development and our Organizational Strategies, Forms and Leadership[138]:

In these workshops (trainings/ conversations)- we took time to share (in class, in meeting) the State of the World we see ourselves today in, - the politics- , the economy- , societies- , technologies- , trends and so on- including the rise of population, income, including the growth in balance of energy supplies and demands.

These classes were populated with professionals from the integrated energy industry [139]- from well to wheel, and from mill to socket- and from around the world- so we have learned quite a bit from each other along this way.

So- the simple question today is: How are we going to do it?[140][141][142]

During these conversations on Energy Architecture Development , I also started to speak about the opportunity of connecting some dots between the opportunities in the Economy (Economy Transition), the Jobs and Labor markets with that of

---

[137] Nyenrode Business University, Energy Delta Institute, Oslo BI, Trinity College, Columbia University, etc. Etc.
[138] See Global Energy Change Challenge and some presentation material
[139] (oil, gas, utility, distribution, renewable, finance, state, cities planners, architects, consumers, etc.)
[140] See Global Energy Challenge
[141] IN these conversations- we used some energy business model applications, including energy strategy and scenario planning methodologies from the Shell Group.
[142] In this conversation "Small Tales of Conversion" I will not go in detail on how and with what strategies and organizational changes we may attain this. I will and share this in a follow-up dialogue and workbook, specially prepared for the Energy Professionals.

co-investments from the Energy sector and that of the UN Sustainable Development[143], including Paris Climate Change agreement.

But let's look at some numbers, first:

Presently there are currently 7.7 million jobs in clean energy worldwide, according to the Renewable Energy and Jobs 2015 Annual Review by International Renewable Energy Agency (IRENA).

This equates roughly to the number of jobs in the *global* oil and gas sector.

The clean energy sector will continue to grow.- and has as such a vast potential and large space for job creation.

As is currently contributes (only) 3-4% of total world energy and in the next 15 years, projections are for it to grow to 30-40%, so there are tremendous investment and growth opportunities in this sector that will also lead to new jobs.

A recent analysis by UN FCCC/Bloomberg concludes that the world will require $17 trillion USD in new renewable installation costs, in order to move the world into a path of a 2 Degrees Celsius scenario (2035-2050).

The International Energy Agency projects further that the world will need to invest over $50-60 trillion in energy investments over the same period (approximately $2 trillion per year going forward).

Both of these numbers are huge, and we are not preparing ourselves enough to meet them.

Both plans and both of these numbers- and let us please understand that as well- don't jive well together.

Let me explain:

How realistic are the above numbers if we are asked to achieve a 2 degrees Celsius goal?

How can the established oil, gas and coal sector still so much to grow (as it presently does (!) and further according to IEA and BP) and as we today have already crossed and reached 400 ppm of CO_2 in our atmospheres?

How can we grow and transform the energy sector such that we can provide energy and comfort to all people of this world, and whilst maintaining eye on our planetary boundaries?

We are best to understand that we are yet in a very huge gap between what is required, what is today realistic, what is idealistic, what needs changing and what is in spin.

---

[143] See Appendix: walking on the path of UN Sustainable development goals

And let's look now a little bit at the plans for Sustainable Development:

Erik Solheim, present SG of UNEP, a be-friended relation and good optimist, spoke most recently at an annual working conference of Norfund(The Foreign Aid Fund of Norway) [144].He always makes me smile at the (many) positive and enthused examples of "how things are being great and going right".

Erik's opening examples were the history and success stories of Singapore and South-Korea. In addition- and also looking with hindsight over his career- Erik concluded that sustainable development practitioners, governments and businesses now all agree: The idea that (main-stream) business cannot be part of the solution is simply passed .

In fact, and looking at the examples of Singapore and South-Korea (no matter the eco-footprint)- a simple observation can be made:

How to build a nation into prosperity?

Today - three (simple, core and) key ingredients are seen and needed for it's success:

1. Leadership (state/ authoritarian or more benign, inspired and democratic)

2. A vibrant Market--based economy

3. Education

The 'pact' that has being created in the Addis Ababa Finance for Development Conference (Ethiopia)[145] between big-banking (e.g. Sumitomo, Citibank), big-business and (UN) government officials is creating the conditions for private, and mainstream business finance into developing nations- such that this form of magic can be done.

In other words:

Big Mainstream in a Big Sustainable Development Pact- with/from China/BRICS/NDB and also the West.

It is obviously important that we make the better decisions in these Big Mainstream interventions- and truly build the sustainable societies we want and are to last.

Over the course of this working conference day[146]- also some numbers were being shared. I like to quote some of these numbers here - so you get a little bit of a feel in what frame we are - today:

---

[144] Norfund annual conference
[145] Addis Ababa outcome document
[146] Norfund working conference

- *The UN budget is 45 Bn USD every year; The role and function of the UN in our ever more complex world constellation cannot be over-estimated.*

- *The Foreign Direct Investment (Formal Aid) of all our countries to alleviate poverty is about 150 Bn USD per annum.*

- *The same (or a little bit less) is expected from the Finance for development/ Climate Change Negotiations.*

- *Overall- and in aggregate- the world invests 20,000 BnUSD (and growing) in mainstream infrastructure, energy, houses, manufacturing plants, etc. . Every year. Mainstream (Oil, Gas, Coal) Energy takes at least over 10-15 % of this sum.*

- *This size of the global economy is 100 Trillion USD. and again : Mainstream (Oil, Gas, Coal) Energy takes at least 10-15 % of this sum.*

- *The world population is going to 9 Billion People- and with 190 million youth coming out of schools in Sub Sahara Africa- seeking for jobs- every year. The population of Sub-Sahara Africa expected to grow to 2 Billion by mid-century.*

So- the observations can be:

How tiny yet are our contributions to keep our common house in order (peace, human dignity, conflict resolution, climate change, economic stability, sustainability, etc.) in relation to our ever growing main-stream businesses and economies.

How tiny yet our voice to seek a new balance in our ever growing ambitions in our economies, new wealth and power - versus the ways by which we - in aggregate- maintain our house in order- from a natural and sustainability perspective and humanity development (inter-relationship) point of view

How tiny yet the voice of the community leader who embraces community-scaled development versus the mainstream (national and business) drive to build and export urban cities, large corporate businesses, infrastructure, etc.

In honest, we have some serious global and local conversations to do, including a better integration of sector knowledge, plan-making and know-how with the UN Sustainable development goals, including the Paris Climate Change agreement.

The present (integrated, and aggregate of our) economy trends and energy investment programs and numbers today simply don't add-up or make sense. – for our aim of sustainable living.

Fossil energy jobs have traditionally been very lucrative- both to corporate as well to governments, - in taxes, in revenues, in profits and in wages to staff, suppliers and so on. [147]

Clean energy does not have this same mantra.

As we embark on our journey to change our present (fossil fuel) energy-intense driven economies and we aim to grow and re-balance our economies for our societies, we best also are to embrace a plan that can create both energy and non-energy sector jobs.

The transition from an oil and gas economy into a renewable economy will also require altering and transforming other elements of our economy. – to alter the job market, to slow down e.g. some of our more intense industrial-engineering complex, our intensified agriculture(s) and re-balance some of our consuming patterns in city constructions and planning, travel and transport and shopping alike.[148]

To find our better ways to slow down, re-balance and re-direct our attention to provide comfort to *all* people- basically.

In this transition, and in this period of re-balancing- we are asked to care for each other – and allow time and opportunity to transform (converse) and make room for the new.

Sufferings in oil-resource dependent economies, because of the current low price of petroleum in the past year, like Brazil, Nigeria, Russia, and Venezuela- is not a good thing to have - and is best to avoided – for the people in these societies- and during the transition.[149]

As this is a pathway that may lead to revolt, resistance, conflicts and sufferings.

Suffering also takes place when the price of oil is high at $100/barrel and impacts countries that depend on imports, such as India.

---

[147] And this fact is very well understood by the rising fossil fuel and resource holding nations in Asia, African and Latin America (the Global South)

[148] This is specifically relevant in the trade relations from OECD to the rest, and in the South-South co-operation

[149] As those countries are and have been our reliable partners in supplying the fuels of the past (and large part of the first part of this century)- our aim in our international relationship, conversations and management of the transition of the energy sector is best to be one of a shared, soft and wise transition from what is today – till what we do need tomorrow morning

In essence, Governments, (International) Finance and Energy corporations[150] need to become much *better integrated* stewards in and over the planning of a more rapid and steep energy-sustainable economy architecture transition pathways over the next 15 years, the period of the UN Sustainable Development Goals.

A model of energy-economy transition is presently being tested and envisioned by Saudi Arabia (Vision 2030) and that may become an example and of interest to other resource-rich countries, such as Russia, Qatar, Iran, Brazil, Venezuela, etc.

Reality is that we still need to better understand the true impact, intent and results of this proposed transformation in the Saudi Arabia's oil economy, and the effects this has or can have on the international oil commodity trading, speculation of shareholdersvalue in Saudi Aramco, and other unintended consequences that may actually not necessarily help in a peace-ful or tranquil market and fuel transition.

But how do we change the established ways- in companies or national institutions?

Professor John Kotter in "Accelerate – The Evolution of the 21st Century Organization"- argues that we need hybrid organizational forms.

Kotter says that in order to perform to scale, you need hierarchy.

And in order to innovate to scale, you need networked organizations that can rapidly deliver new blueprints for performance delivery in a hierarchy.

Companies like ExxonMobil are currently operating in the hierarchical structure.

What is the role of the global corporates and mainstream economies in the endeavours of community building and attention for the poor?

Let me give an example from the Energy Sector.

First of all- we are to applaud the great work and achievements of the UN Agency – Sustainable Energy For All.

In their words and open invitation to us:

The Sustainable Development Goal 7 on Energy has been set; now it's time to show how to achieve it by 2030. A series of high-level Sustainable Energy for All events around the United Nations Summit (25-27 September) will discuss how to finance, implement and track progress on SDG7. Leaders of governments, businesses, civil society and international organizations are invited to join the thousands of SE4All partners who are already geared up to make sure the Energy SDG succeeds in the crucial years to come.

1. Financing and Tracking Progress of Sustainable Energy for All

---

[150] Multi-national oil and gas companies, state energy companies

2. Role of Partnerships in Achieving Sustainable Energy for All
(co-hosted by the Government of Denmark with SE4All)

3. Achieving Sustainable Development Goal 7 on Energy by 2030: Implementation of Sustainable Energy for All

A couple of simple insights and observations on the general nature of our "change challenge" here:

If you want to help or improve the World (On Energy & Sustainability) - Change Yourself (your company, your nation)[151]

If you want to help the Poor- Change the Rich and the Elite.

Any intelligent fool can make things bigger, more complex, and more violent. It takes a touch of genius – and a lot of courage – to move in the opposite direction." – E.F. Schumacher

It was Kandeh Yumkella- the United Nations Under-Secretary-General and the Special Representative of the Secretary-General for Sustainable Energy for All- who once said:

Giving power (energy) to the poor and deprived- without giving them the means and ways to improve their own lives and incomes (in the ways sustainable and bespoke to themselves) - is not aid or help but is actually extending or increasing the (local) suffering.

So- in our mind- the role and responsibilities for the people and professional

---

[151] And stop finger-pointing to others, or put conditional conditions to your change.

organisations who want and like to participate in the "UN energy for All (Or UN Sustainable Development) [152]" program and initiatives are to have "eyes and ears"- a kind of **sixth sense** and **discernment** - of *how* to lift people out of poverty- and *how* to put power, human dignity and economic possibility (and responsibility) in the hands of those left behind.

A Good Example of how to roadmap this and to give Energy to the Poor- and in our minds- can be found in the recent work of Practical Action Organization:

Go to publication

This form of approach helps to create the *local communities* who can (again) thrive in well-being without being enslaved by obligations of payments or commitments to new roles or tasks (jobs) which does not serve their own lives or community but those who seek rent from cheap labor.

Community and environment *are to drive* Economy- and - not the other way around.

If you want to read some other opinions on this- I suggest you read some of the words of Fayyaz- a Pakistani Professor and ex- UNDP official and May East - an UNITAR Senior Education official:

How to build sustainable societies
Eliminating poverty in two simple steps
May East report on Brasil

In May's words:

We are taking a different route from the traditional concepts of growth and progress. In our strategy, community and environment drive the economy, not the other way round."
(*my note*: *and of course- if good entertainment and a TV sets belongs to all this- let it be!*)

Without going into much details-but overall, and in the aggregate of our world energy system - we have written the earlier observations of what we may consider the *better* paths in and over our decision making over coming decades:

---

[152] Or UN Sustainable Development

Can our next generation work with this?

Extensive and sufficient studies have been made into the characteristics of the different generations in the workplace and how the Millennial generation is looking for meaningful work where they can make a real contribution in solving the challenges that are being faced by the world.

Different generations asks for different organizations, and different ways of going about building, creating and committing to meaningful work, life and impact.

Most recently and in Oslo, the home of the Nobel Peace Prize but also the Oslo Business for Peace Award. – a new business worthiness pledge for businesses has been initiated and to help " Big Business" to better commit to support the United Nations Sustainable Development Goals.

We have come a good way- but we still have a long way to go .

In my working practice[153], we seeks to help our customers to build from Hope, to become Congruent and to Organize the *system and organizational* changes needed and *truly* integrate the Paris Agreement/ UN sustainable development agenda in the better energy architecture, societal transition and country developments.

In the East and in the West. In the North and in the South.

We understand that every Nation, every Company and every Leader has his own history, culture and natural needs for progression.

It is our view that every Nation would benefit if it would develop its own National Compact[154]- between Government and Corporates, including the international trade relations, and in order to plan and program the implementation of the Paris Climate Change Agreement and UN Sustainable Development- as the leading guide for an integrated governance over the economy and transition management.

In other words:-

So- *developing and investing in* an (national/ local) National Compact becomes a little bit more than only *investing or developing* a point-solution, or the supply side, be it the industry or government side of the equation.

Investing in the Transition now becomes **a 17-dimensional frame[155]**, and whereby the stewards and stakeholders carefully review the best places to invest (or change) their time, money and resources in – in the community- and in order to achieve the best possible impact and sustainable conditions for the relevant economies and societies – not only for the short-term, but for the years to come. And not only for the own location- but also taking the needs and demands of others and elsewhere in considerations.

---

[153] Energy For One World
[154] UN Global Compact. National Sustainable Development Plan: Coa-lition of the willing
[155] The UN Sustainable Development Goals

This new balance in investment and development in and over an Sustainable Development Architecture[156]- asks (government and business boardrooms) to change focus from a sole supply-sided focus (traditional) or business-to-business towards a much more balanced approach including into the realms of Economy, LifeStyle and the construct of sustainable houses and cities.

And in this world of And-And - the players in the Sustainable Development Architecture value chain sit (willingly) around the table, to better share and integrate their investment and development portfolio's towards the best viable and sustainable architecture development concepts and solutions. [157]For the whole.

Not only a private business matter, not only a pure-state or free market play, not a play of state and governance.

It is truly a new public-private compact.

Governance & Geo-Politics	Corporate Leadership	Society amd Corporate Social Responsibility
Market Constellations, including Trade and Commerce	**Sustainable Development Architecture**	Sustainable Development Goals
Legal, Policies and Frameworks	Science & Technology	Economy, Finance and Responsible Investment

And that is a little bit different game than the traditional games that are being played in the silo's of the established large-scale corporates – today- be it in state hands or in public listed company firms.

So :

Our today and tomorrow's economy landscape asks and invites us actually to re-invent ourselves and to become a little bit more imaginative and servant in our

---

[156] A Sustainable Development Architecture includes all components and stakeholders for making the plan. It+s the hard- and soft- sided organizational structure and rules of the constellation a nation sees itself in.
[157] Examples of where this process has been done are e.g. the EnergyWende of Germany or some of the smart Cities built in China and now also India

working approaches and business collaborations in order to empower our societies and sustain our near future.

The new role of the Leadership (in Business and in Government) envisioned is to become the new stewards, the new orchestra leaders- over these 17 dimensions.

The way this (actually) works ("what the top essential needs are" and "big improvement and change drivers are") are different in Rwanda, Ghana and Nigeria- are different in Argentine, Mexico or Brazil, US or Europe, Pakistan, India or Bangladesh than Saudi Arabia, Emirates or Egypt, Turkey or Indonesia, Vietnam and China.

That we know.

This form of Stewardship over the (Integrated) UN Sustainable Development Architecture is not only a new balancing act between Economy, Society, Sustainability, Technology and our International relationships (on location, in the region).- but also asks us to rapidly adapt a better tone of voice and method of collaboration across the value chains of our leading corporations.

And no one is saying that *it is easy*.

If you want to read more on our working approach and considerations:

Go an read our working practice contributions to Energy Architecture and the Sustainable Development Goals: Lets Get Started!

Around the world- *millions and millions* of people are contributing- *every day*- with their souls, hearts and minds - making our world a better place.

For their children and for the generations to come.

Locally, regionally and for some of them- more Globally orientated.

As these people of good will understand it is "not good enough" to wait and see, and all these people of good will understand that the present incumbent organisations are yet not so much ready or fit for the required changes at hand..

Some of *"the change challenges"* we face today - are so engrained in some of the deeper cultural DNA-grains of our social fabric- that they may appear a little more hard to de-code or crack.

(Just think for a moment how the more hard-nosed energy industry-, finance- , military-, and political theatres in countries as wide and diverse as US, Russia, India, China, Saudi- and NW Europe (e.g. Germany, UK, Netherlands...or Norway... actually work- and you will know with me ....and you will come to see with me)

Simple reality is- that by becoming *inspired* and *free* - we may allow ourselves to better *see.*

It is in this *inspiration* and *freedom of mind,* and the *warmth of our hearts* that we can assure ourselves that we are on the proper way- and that we will see the better chances and changes coming our way..

We don't need to hurry. We don't need to worry.

We are on our way.

Inspired- we can walk in beauty.

Transformation of Economy

About the author

Julie A. Nelson is a Professor of Economics at the University of Massachusetts in Boston, a Senior Research Fellow at the Global Development and Environment Institute, and a dharma teacher in the Boundless Way Zen School. She is the author of *Economics for Humans* and many other books and articles which examine the relationship of economics to feminism, ecology and ethics.

(from opendemocracy)

Many of us, informed about world events and motivated by love and compassion, feel the need for profound economic transformation. We started long ago to question injustice, consumerism, and military-industrial ties. The growing specter of climate-change related disruptions has convinced even more people that 'business as usual' is not a viable option.

But what form should this transformation take, and how can we make it happen? I believe that insights from the careful study of both economics and Zen Buddhism can help us along this path—no matter what faith tradition we come from (if any).

I began studying social science, and eventually earned a PhD in Economics, because I thought these studies might help me to contribute to solving the problems of global poverty and hunger. I began studying Zen because—as is a common story—my life was a mess and I needed to find a better way to be in the world. But what drew me further into both endeavors was the way in which Zen *and* social science (though not, unfortunately, the discipline of economics) encouraged me to entertain doubt, and try to look afresh at the world with a 'don't know mind.'

My economics classes taught me that self-interest and competition rule economic life; that the purpose of firms is to serve their shareholders; and that capitalist economies must grow without limits. These are treated as fundamental principles or even 'laws.' I have found these tenets reiterated by many progressive activists, Buddhist scholars among them. David Loy, for example, repeats these beliefs on Transformationin writing about the Three Poisons of greed, anger and ignorance as being institutionalized in our economic system.

In thinking about economies and well-being from this perspective, the route to transformation looks obvious: if the present system institutionalizes the wrong values, then clearly we need to dismantle it and create a replacement economy. This new economy should be founded on the diametrically opposite values of compassion, cooperation, community, and sufficiency. Many activists seem to feel very certain about this conclusion.

But, using my 'don't know' mind, I became curious about how economists discovered these principles and 'laws,' and I found that they weren't discovered through research at all. Instead, economists *made them up.* Wanting to emulate the 'hard' sciences, they took the complex, emergent, social interaction we call the 'economy' and stripped off all its human dimensions. Then they analyzed this desiccated, distorted model using physics-like concepts of 'laws' and 'forces.' So the image of the market economy as a machine that functions according to universal laws was created by economists who were seeking professional prestige.

I also compared these beliefs about fundamental principles to basic Buddhist tenets, and found that they came up very short. People have now become so used to thinking of the current economy as *essentially* characterized by profit-making, self-interest, and competition that they no longer notice that this is a manufactured image. Yet one of the central teachings of Buddhist philosophy is *anatta,* or 'no-self,' which means that all phenomena lack any essential nature. Another is *anicca,* or the impermanence of all things.

In Zen meditation practice, one learns to question the idea that there is a personal, on-going, separate-from-others 'me' that has unchanging characteristics. But if *all* things lack an essential nature and are constantly changing, this must also be true of economies. Like everything else, economies arise from a flux of contingent, historical, and interdependent phenomena.

So both the study of the history of economics and the study of Buddhism leads us to be skeptical about the supposed laws and principles that underlie the current economic system. Taking a fresh look at real world evidence should further weaken their hold on our imaginations.

Consider, for example, the common belief that the essence of a corporation is to make money for its shareholders. This idea is not based in law (despite a widespread belief that this is so), nor was it derived from the observation of actual businesses. Business leaders actually have quite a lot of leeway in what they do—for good or ill.

In any business journal you can read about corporations that are more oriented towards innovation (like Google), or expansion like (Amazon), or maximizing CEO compensation than they are towards shareholder value. Others actively try to contribute to a sustainable world or make their business a force for good. Most have several goals, among which profit is only one. Still others are a mess and don't seem to pursue any goal effectively at all.

Relentless profit maximization wasn't the only myth invented by economists. The 'free market,' 'imperatives to grow,' 'perfect competition,'and the idea that economies can function without widespread norms of cooperation and trust were also invented. Authors such as Yves Smith and Lynn Stout show clearly how selfish opportunism—far from being *necessary* for economic functioning—actually *destroys* economic systems and corporations. My own work on Economics for Humans delves deeper into the actual necessity of joining economics with care.

Likewise, Buddhist teachings should help us to relax our tight grip on the image of the ideal 'replacement economy.' If we imagine that the new economy will have a good essential nature, we deny *anatta.* If we envision the replacement economy as an end point or culmination of the search for social justice, we deny *anicca*—the inescapability of impermanence and change. If we place our hopes in an idealized end to suffering (or *dukkha*), we deny the teaching that tells us that suffering is a basic feature of existence.

Relaxing our belief in essences also leads to a different interpretation of The Three Poisons: greed, anger, and ignorance. The Sanskrit word for ignorance, *moha*, is sometimes translated as 'certainty.' The more certain we are about something—like the 'essential'nature of the current economic system—and the more we resist looking at it with a 'don't know' mind, the more deluded we can become.

Anger is also a clear temptation if we buy into the replacement economy model. It's very easy to see ExxonMobil, for example, as motivated by greed, and our own anger as righteous. Yet Buddhist teaching reminds us that anger is a poison and that 'us versus them' thinking arises from a deep delusion of separation. If we see people 'inside the system'—especially 'corporate elites'—as no more than weak, deluded, role-playing robots, we deny them their humanity.

And if we think that *we*aren't motivated by greed, we deny *our*own membership of the human race. Greed for money is only the least subtle variety of this vice. I want climate change to stop along with child abuse, unemployment, sexism, racism, war, the arms trade, and nuclear weapons. Yet with a little introspection, I've realized that I don't just simply aspire to relieve suffering—I have additional desires (demands really) that I pile on top of that aspiration: 'I want to feel good about myself' 'and 'I want to be free of guilt.'

While feeling myself to be part of a righteous vanguard could feed these ego needs, they are precisely the sort of deluded self-making that Buddhism warns about. Suffering arises when we feel that the world is unsatisfactory and should conform to our wishes. Wanting the world to be this way so that I can always feel righteous and effective is a very subtle form of greed, but it is greed nonetheless.

To address the suffering arising from economic problems we need changes in our hearts, and then we need to take these changes out into the world. Just because we don't need a wholesale replacement economy doesn't mean that we don't need structural and systemic changes. Within any nation, community or organization there are forces that shape the flows of information, values, decisions, and patterns of activity that underpin economic institutions, so that's where there are huge opportunities for action.

Economies, markets, and corporations, like human individuals or any other institutions, arise contingently, historically, and in deep interdependence with one another. Recognizing this fact opens up many possibilities for wise, compassionate, pragmatic, and deeply engaged action, not in some imagined alternative universe but in *this* messy and painful world. Letting go of the image of economic transformation as a gigantic battle between two opposing sets of principles frees us to work on cultivating good wherever it can spring up, and disarm evil in whatever forms it emerges in the here-and-now.

This article is based on a talk (video, text) given at the Harvard Divinity School and sponsored by the Religions and the Practice of Peace Initiative on February 18, 2016.

Chapter 4: The Bridge

Three-in-One Living Leadership

Let's look at some of these learnings and insights of how the Living Church has been organized, and created- and translate this into our world of professional Leadership over Business and Governance (Governments), or e.g. Theory U.

Well-a couple of observations– may help us on our inventory and journey:

-   The Living Church is for and by its People.

-   The Living Church is based on a deep felt and connected story- of value and values- that is believed and hold true over a long (longer) period of time

-   The Living Church is led by Living Leadership- that knows-how to attune and reform the tradition and organization to the needs of today and tomorrow.

Let me call this here: "Three-in-One" Living Leadership.

So- how does this relate to e.g. modern change leadership theories such as e.g. Theory U of the theorist and university lectorer Otto Scharmer of MIT?

Well- long story short:

Of course there is some resemblance and overlap with the story and research of theorist Otto Scharmer on the ways by which societies, organizations, or bureaucracies can come to presence a change in innovation or strategic direction..

But the theoretical models of and from organizational change science experts[158] may lack some essence.

Actually the "real-deal".

The "real-deal" of "Living Leadership" and the more inspired "Process of Atonement and Conversion".

Let me briefly explain:

So- whilst I will or cannot claim of course the overall organizational leadership success of and by the Church (or any other religion or faith leadership), what I can share and mention is the honest time taken for inspiration[159] and the more

---

[158] leadership of change at business management schools
[159] Prayer, meditation, contemplation

deep and heart-felt surrender to a call for duty and mission, as and when seen or received from above.[160]

This it not only captured recorded in the lives and stories of the Saints of the Church, this is actually the process of religious (atonement and) conversion experienced by every man and woman of faith and good will.

In Gandhi's words:

If you want to change the world- start by yourself.

And for People who have made an effort to understand Gandhi's or Mandela's life, -will know and may have come to see – of what a moral struggle, journey and time it has taken them to become the men that was required to make and set India and South Africa free.

These were almost journeys of carrying a cross.

It is this conversion process – these true journeys and moral influences- that can help us in our process of *true* reforms.

But this "real-deal" reform is not a simple step-program, individual or in team[161]- but is more a way of life, a passion, that has been with us – for well over 2000 years.

Modern days styled organizational change theories[162] are at times a little shallow and easy on these intricacies of our human development, and forego some of the human complexion [163] and the great many challenges we may see and find on our ways into realizing the UN Sustainable Development goals.

And we *know* that today we are in an ever more complex, and dynamic geo-political, economic and social situation as we have *ever* been or seen before, so our deepening of the "real-deal" is perhaps a better strategy and remedy to our avail, then a simple and (corporate leadership) feel-good formula on paper, and from a strategy or corporate communication department.

I pledge here to keep our eyes open and available to *what is the real deal*, and what our world today *actually* invites and *asks*, and *may need* from us- to consider and become.

---

[160] It is a fact that the Church has had now some decades of faltering attention, scandals, drop in membership and attendance, especially in Western Europe and the Americas. The onset of mass secularization has led to the emptying of Churches and the sharp decline in Priests ordinations. The average age of the Clergy in the Church of NW Europe is 65 years. To that end – the call for new Living Leadership can also be asked from the present Church. Re-build my Church!

[161] A simple organizational change intervention

[162] E.g. Theory U, Otto Scharmer
.

From the Story of a Saint to the Story of a Global (Planetary) Consciousness movement.

Leadership, Priests and Ambassadors

The quest we find ourselves in- of attaining Sustainable Development between each other, today- does not ask for a single individual or national strong leadership, and en-lighted person or country, or the story of a single Saint.

Nor are our modern times expecting to see that building and shaping our future and the roads are all so self-evident or can be encaptured by a single group or a single approach and style.

Nor do our times invite us to re-invent the wheel. A new world order. A new organization, a new leadership model that can or may be able to do it all.

We are living in a day and time, of an ever inter-connected world, and where the better ways for organizing ourselves will and can be cross borders, cross silos and cross working interests.

What our quest for Sustainable Development does invite and ask is to see ourselves mobilized into a new movement.

A movement of inspired leadership.

A movement of more planetary conscious leadership

A movement of the Spirit of Assisi (Peace and All Good)

And a movement with ambassadors and priests that can cross bridges, cross polarizations and divides and bring unity in diversity. Bring sustainability and integral human development as a centre piece of our future fit.

A movement that is "fit" to connect some dots, and a movement that is properly inspired to build the future we want.

Was the (Godly) question posed to Saint Francis some 800 years ago:

Re-build my Church.

Today, the question, and as also seen by Pope Francis is:

Please protect and preserve My World and help the rise of an integral human development

Re-build My World[164] (Laudato Si!)

---

[164] Build Paradise on Earth

In order to do so, we know that we are on a path and journey that asks and invites us, to:

Reform our Economies

Reform our Business and Government Governance and Operating Models- Global, Regional and National

Reform of our international trade relations and the way we integrate sustainable development (and integral human development) in the ways we live, work and breathe.

Reform the ways we apply science and technologies: better navigated and better servant to Life and Creation: the more higher form of integral human development[165].

And indeed –

It will also ask to:

Reform (or Put some new Flames of Fire[166]) in the Church and its relationships with societies, including the interfaith peace building dialogue

Reform and create a better balance between Politics, Business, Science and Religion in our future decision making.

A re-newal and refreshing of the role and responsibilities of Spiritual leadership (Religion, The Church) in and over the more worldly powers: Government and Business Leadership

A new balancing act.[167]

And a movement that includes both Priests, Business and Government Leadership, Scientists, and practitioners and the people that represent Nature and the integral human development (Societies).

I call it our St. Francis 2.0.

So "Living in this Movement" for the true attainment of the Sustainable Development invites us to build Living Organizations and Relations that can.

Remember the Three-in-One of the Living Church.

Now – the good news is:

---

[165] Moral ethical codes of the application of science and technology and in relation to life and Creation.
[166] E.g. Opus Dei, Franciscan OFM, Jesuits,
[167] Whilst in the religion of Islam this re-balancing may actually asks for another kind of reform of the role, interpretation and position of religion, than which is relevant for the Church. So here again: different countries. Different religions. Different rebalancing.

If one decide to make him or her available for this journey of Peace and All Good,

Living from this One Heart, - or this deep-felt wish to see Humanity live in Peace and Understanding- does something to the Human Being.

It opens our Collective Hearts.

And it opens our Collective Minds and Souls to some new and fresh imaginations and callings.[168]

---

[168] To that end, the theorist Otto Scharmer has a little bit of right- after all.

Fictional Tales of Conversions of Nations.
(from Empire Era to Planetary Consciousness)

Let me conclude this booklet with some (fictional) examples of how our nations could find themselves inspired by the invitation from Pope Francis and the UN Sustainable Development Goals, and see themselves on the path of conversion and convergence towards a more planetary conscious, including a better balance between human formation, ecology and economy development.

These conversions from Empire era to a much more harmonic Planetary consciousness doesn't come by itself, but will truly require the eyes and minds of Awakening and the Leadership skills be-fit to move away from what is today- till what we would like to see, experience and aspire for our tomorrow.

As our world is accelerating and becomes ever so much more a complex bee-hive place of diversity, complexity, connectedness, ambitions, and urgencies in our social, economic, financial and political lives, the invitation and the "duties of care" put on ourselves is not for the meek, but truly asks for courage, imagination, creativity, stewardship and skills.

As it is today already quite a skill to maintain the present (national) operating – political, government and corporate business system(s) working, we actually seem to have little time to think and reflect a little deeper- and see the consequences of our today's intra-nation systems and daily actions on the longer time-frame, nor do we take the time to imagine and experiment enough with making room for the new.

Making "room for the new" – in our overly systemized bureaucracies- simply does require effort, creativity and inspiration.

A simple mantra in use in present day leadership (training) – both in government administration as well in business is the following:

If it is working, and it ain't broke- don't fix it

When there is a crisis, just keep your heads-down and keep working at it

We don't need (Policy) Visions. We just need keep working and staying out of trouble

Very generally speaking, these forms of operational credo's has taken form and root in Presidential Offices and Boardrooms alike , over the last decades[169][170], and are – again very generally speaking- valid in the more state-led economies as well in market-based economies[171].

---

[169] in the East and in the West
[170] e.g. also a result of the Financial Crisis of 2008 and low-economic growth/ low oil prices of 2015-2016
[171] e.g. aftermath of the Financial Crisis of 2008

As present days and times can feel pressing, - with simply overwhelming agenda's and a sheer amount of administration,

with job duties and cares, financial and performance delivery targets, global and local market changes and competitions, national debts, and monetary crisis, social issues, global or more local conflicts, rivalries for position, national re-elections or re-organisations and so on-

It requires insights and eyes on essences in order not to fall in the trap of re-active management, but stay on course for Pro-active Governance and Visionary Leadership.

Re-directing the course of a Nation, is like being a captain of a large super-tanker wanting to change course.

It takes time. It takes patience. It takes skills. And it requires a New Soft-Tuned Navigational Operating Guide.

The re-direction of a Nation asks for inspiration, vision, persistence, re-organisation and the build-up of momentum and organisation of capabilities[172] – attuned between the established organisational forms and formats in business, in government and with their societies- and in order to achieve and succeed over longer period of times.

The re-direction of a Nation asks and invites us to transcend a little from our own working and political interests and to learn better to converse and converge short-term political opportunistic behaviours into true opportunity and vision (dream) building with the more longer-term wave and impulse[173]:

1. What role and function can our Nation play in the build-up and realisation of a more Planetary consciousness?

2. What duties of care do we have in our own Nation to further and advance the human development, ecology and economy balance- such that the Nation can truly become a Sustainable society (UN Sustainable development Goals)

3. What can we do for our Neighbours and other Nations, and how best can we organise our national (organisational capabilities and) outreach and trade relations such that we make a positive contribution to the rise of Nations, and the attainment of UN Sustainable development, including Peace and All Good?

4. How can we bring about and organize these changes- Top-Down and Bottoms-Up – with our local, regional and federal government and business

---

[172] Forms and Formats between Government, Business, Science, Religion and Society

[173] E.g. Laudato Si! UN Sustainable development goals, The Spirit of Assisi, Interfaith peace building and shared planetary consciousness

administrations- in check and attuned - to the directional change we aim to achieve?

It can only come about as part of a long-wave resonance and impulse[174]- which can stand the test of times.

It can only come about if the people of the Nation are touched by their hearts, and feel inspired by this invitation and call for this form of National change.

It can only come about (well) if the aspirations of change and conversion are a natural and logic component of the history, culture, elite and establishment, but include dire considerations for the invitation to "make room for the new" be-fit to a *better* Planet and *better* Life for all.

It can only come about if the general population, government administration and economic business community feel safe and secure, nationally and internationally, such that time and attention can be given to advance and converse today's.

Generally speaking, change comes best when we know how to address a couple of very simple, but essential ingredients, for the journey of change:

1. What shadow sides in our present Establishment and National Operating Theatre (*system*) do we like to heal, change, improve or make better?
2. Where do we see we can make room for the new in our National Operating System for human development, ecology and economy balance, growth and improvements?
3. What goes well and can we celebrate, and what deserves our every attention?

It's almost like human psychology. It's almost like sports championship training and coaching.

And in this journey of analysis, training and inspiration- we *see* well when we know how to attune the Body, the Mind and the Soul of the Nation with the aspirations and conversions and shared convergence, "the Star", we aim to reach.

Pope Francis encyclical Laudato Si! can be an inspiration for these forms of better dialogues and conversations- to blueprint these new workable policies, government administration strategies and business plans that can help to roadmap this journey- and bring the conversion and this convergence about.[175]

The UN Sustainable Development Goals and Agenda is another form and platform asking and inviting us to do so.

---

[174] E.g. Laudato Si! UN Sustainable development goals, The Spirit of Assisi Interfaith peace building and shared planetary consciousness
[175]

The essence of the conversion from a more Empire Era towards a Planetary Conscious National Operating System is not an easy one.

Not when the times are hard or demanding, and not when life is a party and people like to entertain.

But the decision to start on this journey can be made by *every* citizen, *every* politician, *every* government official and *every* business boardroom director, around the world, *right as we speak.*

Of course the attentions of the governments of least developed or rapid developing nations is and are to be different than those who are presently leading in human and economic development.

But the essence remains the same: to foster a spirit of brother-sister companionship, cross-cultures, cross-race and cross-national boundaries and that truly helps to integrate the nation as a member of the rise of planetary consciousness, stewardship over human dignity and nature, and the taking care of the Common Home (Creation).[176]

In the more longer-wave change programs[177] we have come to *learn, see and understand* that discipline, passion and fun are not each other enemy: in essence- and if we aim to achieve a change and conversion program in our society over a longer period of time (5-10 years), then our aim is to build-in enough "carrots and low hanging fruits" such that the conversion can be carried out, followed-through and is attractive to all

My practice experience with Energy Architecture Transition working programs are excellent examples of how national economic and societal (sectorial change programs) can be organised and led by this better form of integrated governance and care.

Extend this to the whole of society, economy and ecology- and you may appreciate with me- the dimensions of the landscape we find ourselves in.

Of course, I am also very much aware of "the pendulum at swing" and the workings of more nationalistic (populism) sentiments[178] with that of a more global humanity and planetary consciousness-

Let us please understand: we are a world in transition, and - in transition- we can see and find ourselves in the eye of the storm, in the storm or having achieved or set our Sails on the New Land and Shores.

---

[176] It has been St. Francis and the present St Francis FMO order that proofs that povery and planetary consciousness are not each other enemy. The contrary is in this case actually true: by adopting the vow of poverty, the Saint Francis order has found and received grace for a extra-ordinary level of spiritual consciousness and human awareness, in grace.

[177] Corporate

[178] Me First

But what I do know is:

If we don't dare to become ourselves the ones that choose to cross this Storm and Blue Ocean[179], how else can we hope to arrive at the new Shores?

And again with Gandhi:

> *"You must be the change you want to see in the world."*

Let me now try to paint you a couple of (fictional) conversations that we may see and hear when we start to move from empire to planetary- and look at our own nations with a little different lens and view:

---

[179] This word is here also used symbolically. Blue Ocean strategies has become a known term in use in the international business community.

"America Exceptionalism" not such a good idea, not for our better tomorrow

It's obvious. It's clear.

Claiming our Exceptionalism in a world where everybody longs for his or her own dignity, respect and rightful place, is no longer such a good idea.

Yes- we are a great country, but so are so many others (if not all) also.

It is when I changed my own minds and views, and start to see the world as an interconnected whole, that I ever become so much more aware of our own humble place on planet Earth (we are only with 350 million people).

It is when I changed my own minds and views that I became also aware of some of the shadow-sides of my nation, and that has imprinted so much on our world today.

Let us agree that the consuming patterns of our average American family is way beyond what our Planet sustainably can carry.

Let us also agree that the ways we have exported our business cultures has done really some good, but has also been the cause of much of the McDonaldfication, digitalisation and commercialisation troubles of societies around.

Our society, our nation, is just a little bit odd with the "green back" : money has become too important in our society: in our governments, and in our businesses.

I feel personally very sorry for that.

On the military I feel personally a little mixed. Whilst it is or can be hold true that we have helped to liberate or maintain peace and order over some turbulent decades and years, ever since world war II- I am a little concerned with the intensity and the enormity of the ever galloping weapons industry and what this may bring to future generations:

If we are going to use all these advanced weaponry and robotized warfare tools- who else is going to do and use this over the next decades? And with what consequences?

Personally, I believe our coming century deserves our every attention for the demilitarization of our and all nations.

I am also a little disappointed that we are yet to find a better balance between our diplomacy, military and our actually more positive active nation and peace building[180].

---

[180] UN Sustainable development

I feel we have a blind spot on international and cultural subtleties and nuances, and have yet something to learn.

This has been true in Vietnam, Korea, Iraq, Afghanistan, Libya, Syria and so on.

We have got a lot to learn, as we also have a lot going for us.

Yes.- I really like our optimism, our generally speaking positive can-do, and our ways of going about the more practical things: Americas great inventors, entrepreneurs and big dream politicians and international change leaders, such as Martin Luther King, Kennedy, Reagan, Clinton, Obama and so on.

We have done and accomplished a lot.

I believe America (we) is and can become an even more important part of the puzzle that can help our world future further-

Yes I believe we in America can start and become a very good member of this New Planetary Dream of Conversion and Convergence.

Saudi and Dubai Riches no longer so cool

It took us quite a while to come to Assisi. We are simple too busy. Too busy with minding my hotels, businesses and new start-ups

Yes- we in Saudi and Dubai, we have take extra-ordinary steps to allow for the rapid creation of new businesses and dreams for our society and youth.

Under the wise and visionary leadership of our King Salman and Sheikh Rashid Al-Maktoum – Dubai has now e.g. an under-minister of Happiness, as we have a new drive and vision for making our countries the centre of world business, innovation, sustainability, entertainment and peace.

Our education and cultural programs are excellent and have become second to none.

We are truly on top of the world.

Nevertheless all that-we feel that we were maybe something lacking- in the cosmopolitan development of Dubai specifically or that we had a cultural (interfaith) blind spot for what is needed or may be coming.

Then we observed this 4-days interfaith business & spirituality retreat possibility in Assisi- and which further programmed a more in depth conversation on Laudato Si and the UN Sustainable development Goals.

And to our surprise- we are taken.

We are taken what this has personally meant to us, as we have been given an insight I believed was not possible.

Let me explain

Abundance and Richness are generally seen in our faith as a blessing of God (Allah)- for work well done.

But by being in contact and dialogue and conversation with my peers in class in Assisi, the program, and the deep spiritual conversations also with the Friar Minors of the St. Franciscus order- we have seen a new interpretation and new reality in this message of our beloved prophet Mohammed.

Care for the Common Home and Creation is a shared theme and topic in all religions.

As such- the call of Pope Francis to better care for human development, ecology and economy- in more balance- could have been a call from my Prophet as well any of our religious leaders in our faith.

When this insight sunk a little in into our own thinking and reflections, and as we walked the pebbles and streets of Assisi- something odd started to take hold in us and in our mind:

Of course, and first of all, there is the story of St Francis, a man- who some 800 years ago to decided to change his eyes from attaining material wealth into caring for the poor and deprived.

And to live only for Peace and All Good.

To that end, I am a little saddened how some of (the messages in) my religion, Islam, - which means Peace- has also been made and seen by others in connection with the rise of international terrorism[181] . In fact, a latest article in the New York Times argues that my country is both arsonist and firefighter in this arena. That concerns me, and we should speak a little more on this- what can we together do- to change this ? [182]

But secondly, and in addition- it appeared to us- how the simplicity of the present village and people in Assisi (there are no luxury hotels above 3/4-stars) actually shines on them in beauty and peace – and on all people visiting this somewhat miraculous mountainside township.

How Assisi (and the people of Assisi) is and can be actually another star-example of how we may want to live.

It made us both feel a little nostalgic. And it made us remember the early days of our beloved mother lands- when simplicity and beauty were also still very much connected.

The early days of our native and beloved mother lands were the days when we saw ourselves more in community, more in peace, and more in touch with our natural environment.

Now, if I think back of how our present country look like- of course – we are very proud and honour the achievements and guidance of our wise leadership, but we also feel a little awkward to think about all these 5 and 7 star hotels, their swimming pools and their luxury apartments and food.

We personally now feel also a little more attracted to live our life a little more in simplicity, in attunement and in doing good.

---

[181] New York Times article : Saudis and Extremism: 'Both the Arsonists and the Firefighters', August 25, 2016

[182] perceptions

Given the rat-race and rapidizations of our societies, I can see now a new role and function in my life and in our beloved countries:

Helping to nurture this more planetary consciousness, Helping to build more Peace, Growing more subtle care for each other and more care for our beloved planet and nature (also in our energy business).: in a new and more humble form of simplicity and care.

Yes- we can see with some new eyes, and Yes- we are highly inspired to bring forth some good new works that may help to foster this (interfaith) Spirit of Assisi.

Yes we believe that inter-religious dialogue – as proposed and practiced here in Assisi- is more than needed and welcome. Also in our religion of Islam and between our religious leaders, and between the people of good will and faith.

May Allah Bless!

Old Europe's weaknesses – please forgive me- may actually still be a holding place where we can inspire and learn to better live, share and care

Yes- Europe seems to run a little out of steam, these last couple of years. A range of crises[183] has assumed a lot of time and agenda space. But let´s not write-off this Grand Old Lady, nor ignore it´s ever available beauty.

The countries and societies of Europe has still a lot speaking for them. Let me explain:

It was only 3 years ago, that the EU received the Nobel Peace Prize in Oslo, and for the political and social experiment of integration and peace building after the second world war. The commitment and convictions in Europe for freedom of movement, speech, services and goods cannot be ignored or understated. Add to this the levels of maturity, bench strength and resilience of the intelligentsia and general population, including the elites of societies on their global (planetary) consciousness, wish for sustainability and doing well in the Paris Climate Change accords.

Of course this is not always fully carried by their national and political government administration programs, nor by Europe s multi-national businesses that compete internationally.[184]

Europe administration and business community could truly benefit if they were better able and adopting the words and meanings of Laudato Si and UN Sustainable development in their mainstream businesses, government administration and economies.

Nevertheless all that- you can see and witness in Europe the rise of a whole new creative class[185], and that actually is quite active in shaping a new formed network , communities and sharing economy, and that can become exemplary to other countries or blocks.

As such- the richness and diversity of free expression and lifestyles in Europe is and remains a jewel in our cultural diverse world and global civilisation.

Add to this, the general availability of lots' of practical know-how on sustainable energy, sustainable development and sustainable societies, and you know that Europe's future is far removed from her retirement.

Europe however would grossly benefit, if national and more regional governments and administrations – would recognize this new role and

---

[183] E.g. Russia-Crim-Ukraine Conflict, Syria war, (ISIS) terrorism and refugees/immigration, Euro Crisis, Greek Bail-out, Youth Unemployment in Southern Europe, Turkey Coup, Brexit, Nato Alliance, etc.
[184] Some can be seen doing lip-service or window dressing
[185] Approximately 25% of the European Population of 500 Million

opportunity Europe has in the wider scheme of things: to become a laboratory, a program school and a helping agent for the realization of Sustainable Societies.

Less telling. More Listening. Better serving. [186]

The present rivalries and competitions of the national governments of Europe and its' business communities in international trade has better to stop[187]:

Europe would be so much better to the world, if it knew how to better integrate the key and new future values[188] *in her delivery chains in the more serving sustainable development programs- cross countries, cross cultures, cross silo's and cross working interests- and such that true New Bridges of hope, inspiration and conversions can be created from Europe to the Rest of the world.*

A new and shining "Face of Hope" and "Heart of Compassion" in our international family.

I am confident and sure she can.

---

[186] Obviously the historic past of colonialisation and surpression of others (slavery) better in the conscious mind and international relationship habits: truly demonstrating the learnings from past mistakes

[187] It has been a well known joke in the International diplomatic circes of the US and the rest: Who to all when you want to speak with Europe?

[188] In accordante with Laudato Si!

China's Leadership ready for a new phase of Compassion, Freedom and Soul

I think I might state the obvious:

Can you imagine what it takes and how complex a job it is to steer China present economy and society?

The enormity of our country: 1.2 Billion people and growing, and with an economy and manufacturing goods and services capabilities in world reach and scale, now second to none.

How can you lead and manage this?

On purchasing parity and on power of the economy- we are long past Japan, and now soon also USA.

We are simply the greatest and most influential (and hence responsible) nation on Planet Earth.

So- the 21st century will be the century of China. And Asia.

China will assume again its' rightful place in the ranking and positions of nations. Presidents Xi China dream already a reality.

Of course- China is not without its' own growth challenges. We know we have some inefficiencies and political and business corruptions to take care of. We know that we have severe and serious environmental pollutions and damages.

But I have no doubt that our Political Leadership will find the scientific best ways to tackle this and lead China from this course – into more clean and safer havens.

The difficulties in China may actually also be an opportunity.

As I have come to learn of the Spirit of Assisi and Laudato Si!- I actually see something which may become a true new value in our Country Leadership and programs:

How if we learn and know how to bring more compassion, more heart and more soul into the Political Party and our Business Community Leadership?

How if we take the time and learn our present people and our leadership to trust a little more, and to make room for some new freedoms, including inner well-being and freedoms.

How wonderful if China would raise its' care and compassion for every living soul in China, and also that we use this form of new found compassion and heart in our international and overseas exploitations .

The last Olympic Games in Rio showed some of this New Hope, and this longing for a New Spirit in China.

It was Miss Fu Yuanhui- a member of our China Swimming team- that - thanks to her most funny and honest expressions after her swimming contest, and made in plain public, – that changed the eyes of her team and sports leadership.

"Failure is no longer a Shameful word".

Her Honesty, and Miss Fu Yuanhui funny ways of going about things helped our own national (sports-) leadership and our government to relax and relief a bit:

And China (as perhaps the rest of whole world) simply loved (the ways of) Miss Fu Yuanhai.

So- this is truly a form of some New Hope.

Some New Hope- that things can be a bit more relaxed- and less achievement seeking- in China.

As such- we may be encouraged by the present Political leadership choice of making Confucius again a historic leading moral thinker of choice.

Yes- I recognize how difficult it is, and must be to steer a political process attended by the People Representatives in congress- but how wonderful it would be if our leadership relaxed a little more, and took a bit more time to let some of our performance indicators down, and spend a little more time in raising the well-bing of our people: empowering more freedoms in mind, heart and soul.

In essence, and that is what I have seen and experienced in Assisi- it is no longer the material goods or gains that makes us happy: its' actually the freedom and quality of our souls, minds and hearts that makes our life rich and wonderful.

Yes- I hope to see this Spirit of Assisi to take hold in our communist party and in our country and abroad.

As such- we may be encouraged by the present Political leadership choice of making Confucius again a historic leading moral thinker of choice.

Yes- I recognize how difficult it is, and must be to steer a political process attended by the People Representatives in congress- but how wonderful it would be if our leadership relaxed a little more, and took a bit more time to let some of our performance indicators down, and spend a little more time in raising the well-bing of our people: empowering more freedoms in mind, heart and soul.

China a little bit more like Miss Fu.

In essence, and that is what I have seen and experienced in Assisi- it is no longer the material goods or gains that makes us happy: its' actually the freedom and quality of our souls, minds and hearts that makes our life rich and wonderful.

And our Heart-warm Laughing together did some miracles too!

Russia's Bear Heart ready for more caring, soft-natured and subtle Leadership

We Russians, we have a long tradition. But we also look at the world from our country perspective: Our country is the largest country on the Planet. Our country covers 10 (or 11) time zones, and ever so much differences in people, ethnicities and cultural backgrounds.

Nevertheless all that, we can truly speak of One Russia. One Russian Heart and Soul for our country, for our people and for our President.

We are a Nation of Pride.

Assisi (and your team of interfaith peace building) came on my radar- by some surprise.

Ok, it's true that we have some of the largest Oil and Gas companies on the planet: Rosneft and Gazprom.

And thanks to our relationships with the Dutch, and – we were made aware of this special program in Assisi: UN Sustainable Development, Business & Spirituality.

I must admit: I liked it.

Straight away. As a born Orthodox Christian, I have always felt for the holy pilgrim places and shrines, and I like to travel to them, and see them.

But I must admit.

Assisi and the program of the workshops has exceeded all of my expectations.

Actually- it is a small miracle.

It opened my eyes, and it made me really feel proud, humble, almost closer to God.

What I have learned most during my presence in Assisi- is that the way we relate to others, is a reflection of how we are ourselves, and how we relate to God.

Knowing the complexities in my profession (I work with Gazprom), and the difficulties we have to manage that ship in the many gas and working interests we have, around

And knowing how important this income stream is to the State of Russia,

I must admit- I changed my view on some of our importances and some of our relationships. I see now better that integral human and sustainable development is better to include in our mainstream gas business operating model.

Now, and as I have some good relations inside Gazprom and of course our Political Process, and I know for sure- that some of the things we discussed here this week I will bring home, and that will make a difference. Will help us to become a little more open, a little more caring, and little more appreciative of some of the efforts people in the Energy transition/Energy innovation are doing, and perhaps a little more creative in how we can better integrate the strength of the Russian Bear Heart, our Gazprom, into the projects and programs of UN Sustainable Development-

As said- I am very pleased of having found this new dream: of Peace and All Good.

India's rise not to rival China or US, but *just* to Make India Happy in and with the World.

Its rather simple.

Our President Pranab Mukherjee and PM Modi mentioned it – already- in their address to the Nation on the celebrations of our 70th year independence day.

Please make the People of India Happy.

Let me share here some quotes from our President:

- *May our studies be brilliant; may there be no hostility amongst us; may there be Peace Peace Peace.*
- *We are in the process of forging new relationships based on shared values and mutual benefit with all countries.*
- *India's focus in foreign policy will remain on peaceful co-existence & harnessing tech & resources for economic development.*
- *India will grow, only when all of India grows; the excluded ones have to be included in the development process.*
- *It is much more important to look to the future; it is time to join hands to cooperate, innovate and advance.*
- *We cannot call ourselves a civilized society if we fail in providing safety and security to our women and children.*
- *We must take destiny in our own hands to build the India of our dreams.*
- *As we build an India of smart cities, towns & villages, we must ensure they are humane, hi-tech and happy places*

India's development can only be Sustainable Development.

If we, India and the world, fail to discern, frame and realize the more sustainable solutions [189], then the world, and India- will see some (serious) trouble.

India's Developments today is almost a synonym for the (urgent and important) call for Sustainable Development.

Everything being said and done in this booklet, and in our conversations at Assisi, are right.

We have to find the pathways that leads us to a more happy life. We have to curtail some of the ambition levels of some of our elite and corporate leadership, and some of our international expansion programs.

How wonderful if we also work from the bottom of the pyramid, and Make India Happy- and build humane and smart communities to all.

India is not China, nor America

---

[189] On All 17 UN SDGs

India needs to find its' own way of (modern) development- and best if we keep our social fabric peaceful and happy.

To that end, the words and deeds by PM Modi are encouraging:

- *I have tried to adopt the strategy of 'Reform, Perform and Transform'; tried to avoid populism.*
- *The onus is on the 125 crore people of India to convert this 'Swaraj' into 'Surajya'. From Parliament to panchayats, gram pradhans to the prime minister, everyone has to fulfill their responsibilites. Only then will the dream of surajya come true.*
- *Our social unity is most important; division in the name of caste, creed hurts the country. Need to rise above all these issues.*
- *We all have to fight against social evils, have to support social justice. Great leaders like Mahatma Gandhi, Ambedkar ji have always stressed on the need for social unity.*

Yes- It will be good if India can keep its' eyes and ears towards the more integral human and sustainable development.

Temper a bit our national ambition levels and the greed for money and power, and nurture a little more the compassion and care for each other.

It will be very good to boost our (Elite) Leadership Academies of our Youngsters with this message (Spirit of Assisi).

It will be very good if our administration and our powerful business elite could make a National Compact on this.

This will also need to be expressed in our international relationships. Best if Corporates and International Diplomacy is being made clear of this priority:

Please, "Make the People of India Happy"

As we (India) will and can make the world happy..

Are there some other concerns?

Yes- I think in our international politics, our relationships in the region , with e.g. Pakistan, Sri Lanka, Bangladesh, China (Borders) : they are all a little too sensitive these days.

We need a détente.

In addition, we need to maintain an inclusive democracy- where different religions, etnicities and races can live safely and harmoniously together- is also very much of concern and importance, today.

Yes- India can benefit from this Spirit of Assisi. It fits with our Hindu religion and tradition. It includes our Puruṣārthas.

Thank you!

Africa's Pride powered by and for the People

It was a rather small news item in the Economist, but the sad reality today in Africa is that we see some new backslides into more authoritarian leadership styles.

Quote

From the Economist, August 2016

Some call it Africa's second liberation. After freedom from European Colonizers came freedom from African despots. Since the end of the cold war multi-party democracy has spread far and wide across the continent, ofen with impressive and moving intensities.

Many of Africa's worst Big Men (Leaders) were swept away.

And most leaders now seek at least a veneer of respectability, elections have become more frequent and more regular. Economies have opened-up

And yet, African democracy has stalled- or even gone into reverse. Too often, it is an illiberal sort of pseudo-democracy in which incumbent demonises the opposition, exploits the power of the state to stack the electoral contest in his favour and removes constraints on his power.

That bodes ill for a continent where institutions are still fragile, corruption rife and economies weakened by the fall of commodity prices,. For Africa to fulfil its promise, it may want to discover its zeal for democracy.

...

When a country or continents wealth is concentrated in natural resources, controlling the state gives a leader access to the cash needed to maintain power. The problem is aggrevated by the complex, multi-ethnic form of many African states, whose border may have been created by colonial whim. Voting patterns often follow tribe or clan rather than class or ideology, so tend to lock in the advantage of one or other group.

Can the outside world do more than provide African countries with markets? China has become Africa's biggest trading partner, supplying aid an dinvestment with few or no strings attached in terms of the rule of law and human rights. But even China, especially now that its' own economy has slowed, is not in the business of propping up bankrupt African autocrats.

This means that Western influence, though largely diminished, remains considerable- for historic reasons, and because many African countries still look to the West for Sustainable Development investments and sympathy in international lending bodies.

But the West has flagged its efforts to promote democracy, especially in places, such as Horn of Africa or the Sahel.

End of Quote

Do I really need to tell you *how* deeply happy I am, how *truly* thankful and grateful I am with this new initiative from Assisi.

O wow- I am and was so inspired by some of the examples given and discussed: how the more traditional oil and gas sector can become the engine for *the full programming and integration of sustainable development* in the economies and trade relations between my country and the rest of the world.

O wow- how wonderful that we may initiate some new "National Sustainable Development Compacts" for countries such like Tanzania, Kenia, Mozambique, etc. – and better aligned and attuned between the workings of the international (Oil and Gas) corporate community from China , India and the OECD.

O wow- the examples given on how we can better include the voice of the people in the development of local sustainable communities,

I simply loved the example given by you in our workshop of how we may step-up of Jeffrey Sachs'   Millenium Development Villages into Sustainable Communities, around.

The People of Africa *will love* this spirit of Assisi.

Its' our Ubuntu.

Let us shake hands and be glad with it!

And on the Oil & Gas Industry in Africa- Source: PricewaterhouseCoopers LLP (PwC).

"The complexities and challenges facing Africa's oil & gas industry have become daunting. As uncertain regulatory frameworks, taxation requirements and corruption continue to rank at the top of industry's challenges in Africa, it also high time that governments make significant changes."

"Furthermore, players must look at the current state of the industry as an opportunity to reinvent themselves. Given the state of the industry, we think that stakeholders must also consider making changes to their business models. Change is the way to survive in the 'new energy future'. We need to see new business models, new products, new energy sources and new strategies to meet the new reality,"

Concluding Remarks

The booklet "*Tales of Conversion* " is written- for you- and to introduce to you some of the key points of views, insights and perspectives on our Leadership over (UN) integrated Human and Sustainable development- and that may help or support you on your way.

It is in the ways of our Leadership that we may see ourselves to progress the better ways.

It is also to help to raise the conversation(s) we have on said subjects, and to support our shared awareness, insights and sources of inspiration- for our better collective organizations and leadership.

It is by no means exhaustive [190], nor can or does it intend is to be complete.

The booklet is and can only be *our* opening conversation, based on *our* insights and sources of inspiration, gained thanks to my working practice and experiences.

As such – these words desperately needs to become enriched by you and your views on and in this journey,.

Only by an open and honest dialogue, enquiry and conversations between ourselves- on said subjects – can we expect to see ourselves on the better ways.

Changing Lives.

Making the world a better place.

The "*Tales of Conversion* " is rich in examples and case stories- is written in a light and pragmatic way, and will be accompanied by a rich set of presentation material such that it can be used for educational or professional/ corporate outreach purposes.

A rich set of sources, video material and a literature list will accompany the book.

Finally, and not unimportantly, intent of the organization to make ourselves available to support the content of this Booklet and make it "come alive" in presentations, conversations and action agenda's around the globe.

---

[190] I have on purpose kept this booklet brief and thin. In a follow-up workbook, and directed for the Energy and UN Sustainable Development Professionals, I plan to include more applied strategy, organizational change, science & technology, business model and innovation, energy architecture and sustainability process and methodology details- and which can form part of best practices in the field.

Five, Fifteen, 30 Years. Or Tomorrow

This booklet may have been written *too* early.

Maybe – our world is not yet ready or willing to listen to some of the essential views and message(s) included in this booklet: from Prof. Jeffrey Sachs, Pope Francis (Laudato Si!) , Erik Solheim (UNEP), George Soros, etc..

Maybe – our world is doing just fine, happily spinning over coming years.

Maybe our need for an Organizational and Leadership conversion- in and between ourselves and our economies- are just not needed in order to attain thriving economies or sustainable development.

Maybe we don't need to re-image the direction of our global civilisation, nor do we need to re-build the Bridge between Interfaith Peace-Building, The Spirit of Assisi , Laudato Si! and our more mundane mainstream economies and programs under the Paris Climate Change Agreement and UN Sustainable Development in Business and Governments.

It's just "poof".

I personally doubt that.

Maybe – the programs and projects under the Paris Climate Change Agreement and UN Sustainable Development just need *a little bit* of fine-tuning, *a little bit* more time, *a little bit* more commitments , *a little bit* more zippered organizational relationships in order to gain full speed, momentum , global acceptance and uptake,- including *all* the proper, just and fair organizational governance and realizations between the Countries, Businesses and People at hand.

- Renewable energy and new technologies will be the rescuers of our times: they will help, boost and shape our global economies, communities and future into abundance.
- The UN Sustainable Developments Goals will be proven and attained by year 2030.
- The present elected organizational forms and the ways "how we go about our stuff and things" in the G20, UN, individual nations states, our economies, our businesses and other international organizations will govern and do just fine.

Unfortunately- you may doubt this,too- with me.

Maybe in only Five, Fifteen or Thirty Years, - a call is made into Assisi- , and a Peace Building- UN Sustainable Development Leadership Conversion and Intervention is requested by urgent and important matters of State.

A crisis that has "hit the fan".

The UN Sustainable Development goals have come into troubled waters, or – by mid-Century- we see the results of our planetary boundaries *in full sight*.

So, maybe – the use of these words, and the use of the program suggestions are only taken in times of crisis, or in times when the working parties seek redemption and remorse from some of their Leadership acts or oversights

If that were the *only* result of this booklet, believe me, my time and efforts taken *now* – to prepare for this event- has been worth my life and weight in gold,

I would be satisfied.

But maybe- the words in this booklet, and proposed and suggested Leadership Conversion Programs does speak to your imagination, resonate and are seen as "timely and fit".

Maybe you are enthused and inspired, and feel "the positive energy, compassion and power" that can bring timely, true, lasting, subtle, meaningful and caring changes about.

Maybe you feel "this force of good" - and would like to join-in on this mutual discovery process of better attuned leadership for a more and better integral human and sustainable development.

In that case I , and quite humbly, say [191][192][193]:

I am most happy you found me.

You are most welcome.

Please join me on our ways,

Of Building Peace and All Good,

Today. Tomorrow. Always.

May God Bless.

---

[191] With great humility and thanks to the Almighty, Pope Francis, the Catholic Church, The Order of St Francis (FMO), the Spirit of Assisi, the City of Assisi.
[192] With special thanks for hospitality and inspiration rendered by Assisi Mission
[193] Standing on the shoulders of all great women and men that has helped us to form.

Preparing a New Formula for Energy, Paris Climate Change Agreement, and UN Sustainable Development

New opportunities will need to be created with a combination of politics, business, and government and NGOs to help move beyond the more traditional economy and to help businesses and communities create new jobs and opportunities to attain the 17 UN Sustainable Development and Paris Climate Change Agreement goals.

This transition cannot take place overnight.

It will take place in a step-by-step progression. There is an important role here for organizations, and conversations such as this, to help bring about this transition about.

We invite you to join our conversation or contact our working practice. Our mission is to build a community of leaders to enable solutions for a sustainable societies and our world.

Only Peace and All Good.

A New Formula between Energy, Climate & UN Sustainable Development:

Roadmap 2030 =

(Oil & Gas Development) + New Energy Architecture + Finance + Good Stewardship + Jobs in Non-Energy Economy + Paris Agreement + UN SDG 2030.

Follow-up

Open conversation series on this Booklet

This new-styled conversation series is new and fresh and will be launched for the year 2017 and beyond

We are available in *open* conversation/lecture series – and to inspire you, Leaders and Leadership teams, to seek ways to integrate the Spirit of Assisi , Laudato Si! and UN Sustainable Development Goals – in your company, government and organization- and for the attainment of human and sustainable development.[194]

A Pilgrimage into Assisi

A 5-day Business and Government Leadership Pilgrimage program has been specifically designed for Leaders in Business and Government Administrations.

Program of the Pilgrimage combines the contents of this Booklet, the opportunity to meet & greet with the Order (St Francis), the Holy Places and Shrines in the City, the Spirit of Assisi, the Program Makers[195], on location, and to dive deeper into the Bridge between Leadership, Sustainable Development and Spirituality. The essence of this work.

Coaching and Advise

We are available to coach and advice you on your personal and organizational conversion and programs.

We see this as our contribution to the implementation and integration of The Spirit of Assisi, Laudato Si! and the UN Sustainable Development agenda in your local constituency.

Dream Teams

We are available to create with you small, neutral, and independent dream-teams with relevant expertise from around the globe[196][1]- and which may help to "accelerate, diffuse, support " you in the major inspired leadership and organisational conversion and transformational programs- , both in your company as well in your country .
In our frame and realization – we will seek with you the relevant partners- the dream-team so to speak- which can help you in this journey.

---

[194] and to build the value case for business and government administration changes (on location, and in your established constituency) , and to see clear and attractive opportunity pathways forwards, whilst also helping to progress your position and relationships towards yourself, your organization, the stakeholder community and the wider world
[195] Founder(s) Adriaan Kamp and Bente Wolf
[196] spirituality, business, academia, government, etc.

Appendix 1: Laudato Si! – A Map

Laudato si': A "Map"

*This text is a useful guide for an initial reading of the Encyclical. It will help you to grasp the overall development and identify the basic themes. The first two pages are an overview of **Laudato si'** (literally "Be praised" or better, "Praise be to you"). Then for each of the six chapters, there is a one-page summary which gives the argument or main points and some key passages. The numbers in parentheses refer to the paragraphs in the Encyclical. The last two pages are the table of contents.*

An overview

"What kind of world do we want to leave to those who come after us, to children who are now growing up?" (160). This question is at the heart of *Laudato si'* (*May You be praised*), the anticipated Encyclical on the care of the common home by Pope Francis. "This question does not have to do with the environment alone and in isolation; the issue cannot be approached piecemeal".

This leads us to ask ourselves about the meaning of existence and its values at the basis of social life: "What is the purpose of our life in this world? What is the goal of our work and all our efforts?

What need does the earth have of us?" "Unless we struggle with these deeper issues – says the Pope – I do not believe that our concern for ecology will produce significant results" (160).

The Encyclical takes its name from the invocation of Saint Francis, " Praise be to you, my Lord", in his *Canticle of the Creatures.* It reminds us that the earth, our common home "is like a sister with whom we share our life and a beautiful mother who opens her arms to embrace us" (1). We have forgotten that "we ourselves are dust of the earth (cf. *Gen* 2:7); our very bodies are made up of her elements, we breathe her air and we receive life and refreshment from her waters." (2).

Now, this earth, mistreated and abused, is lamenting, and its groans join those of all the forsaken of the world. Pope Francis invites us to listen to them, urging each and every one – individuals, families, local communities, nations and the international community – to an "ecological conversion", according to the expression of Saint John Paul II. We are invited to "change direction" by taking on the beauty and responsibility of the task of "caring for our common home". At the same time, Pope Francis recognizes that "there is a growing sensitivity to the environment and the need to protect nature, along with a growing concern, both genuine and distressing, for what is happening to our planet" (19). A ray of hope flows through the entire Encyclical, which gives a clear message of hope. "Humanity still has the ability to work together in building our common home" (13). "Men and women are still capable of intervening positively" (58). "All is not lost. Human beings, while capable of the worst, are also capable of rising above themselves, choosing again what is good, and making a new start" (205).

Pope Francis certainly addresses the Catholic faithful, quoting Saint John Paul II: "Christians in their turn "realize that their responsibility within creation, and their duty towards nature and the

2

Creator, are an essential part of their faith'" (64). Pope Francis proposes specially "to enter into dialogue with all people about our common home" (3). The dialogue runs throughout the text and in ch. 5 it becomes the instrument for addressing and solving problems. From the beginning, Pope Francis recalls that "other Churches and Christian communities – and other religions as well – have also expressed deep concern and offered valuable reflections" on the theme of ecology (7). Indeed, such contributions expressly come in, starting with that of "the beloved Ecumenical Patriarch Bartholomew" (7), extensively cited in numbers 8-9. On several occasions, then, the Pope thanks the protagonists of this effort – individuals as well as associations and institutions. He acknowledges that "the reflections of numerous scientists, philosophers, theologians and civic groups, all [...] have enriched the Church's thinking on these questions" (7). He invites everyone to recognize "the rich contribution which the religions can make towards an integral ecology and the full development of humanity" (62).

The itinerary of the Encyclical is mapped out in n. 15 and divided into six chapters. It starts by presenting the current situation based on the best scientific findings available today (ch. 1), next, there is a review of the Bible and Judeo-Christian tradition (ch. 2). The root of the problems in technocracy and in an excessive self-centeredness of the human being are analyzed (ch. 3). The Encyclical proposes (ch.4) an *"integral ecology*, which clearly respects its human and social dimensions" (137), inextricably linked to the environmental question. In this perspective, Pope Francis proposes (ch. 5) to initiate an honest dialogue at every level of social, economic and political life, that builds transparent decision-making processes, and recalls (ch. 6) that no project can be effective if it is not animated by a formed and responsible conscience. Ideas are put forth to aid growth in this direction at the educational, spiritual, ecclesial, political and theological levels. The text ends with two prayers; one offered for sharing with everyone who believes in "God who is the all-powerful Creator" (246), and the other to those who profess faith in Jesus Christ, punctuated by the refrain "Praise be to you!" which opens and closes the Encyclical.

Several main themes run through the text that are addressed from a variety of different perspectives, traversing and unifying the text:

*the intimate relationship between the poor and the fragility of the planet,

*the conviction that everything in the world is connected,

*the critique of new paradigms and forms of power derived from technology,

*the call to seek other ways of understanding the economy and progress,

*the value proper to each creature,

*the human meaning of ecology,

*the need for forthright and honest debate,

*the serious responsibility of international and local policies,

3

*the throwaway culture and the proposal of a new lifestyle (16).

Chapter 1 – *What is happening to our common home*

The chapter presents the most recent scientific findings on the environment as a way to listen to the cry of creation, "to become painfully aware, to dare to turn what is happening to the world into our own personal suffering and thus to discover what each of us can do about it" (19). It thus deals with "several aspects of the present ecological crisis" (15).

Pollution and climate change: "Climate change is a global problem with serious implications, environmental, social, economic, political and for the distribution of goods; it represents one of the principal challenges facing humanity in our day" (25). If "the climate is a common good, belonging to all and meant for all" (23), the greatest impact of this change falls on the poorest, but "many of those who possess more resources and economic or political power seem mostly to be concerned with masking the problems or concealing their symptoms" (26). "Our lack of response to these tragedies involving our brothers and sisters points to the loss of that sense of responsibility for our fellow men and women upon which all civil society is founded" (25).

The issue of water: the Pope clearly states that "access to safe drinkable water is a basic and universal human right, since it is essential to human survival and, as such, is a condition for the exercise of other human rights". To deprive the poor of access to water means to deny "the right to a life consistent with their inalienable dignity" (30).

Loss of biodiversity: "Each year sees the disappearance of thousands of plant and animal species which we will never know, which our children will never see, because they have been lost forever" (33). They are not just any exploitable "resource", but have a value in and of themselves.

In this perspective "we must be grateful for the praiseworthy efforts being made by scientists and engineers dedicated to finding solutions to man-made problems", but when human intervention is at the service of finance and consumerism, "it is actually making our earth less rich and beautiful, ever more limited and grey" (34).

Decline in the quality of human life and the breakdown of society: in the framework of an ethics of international relationships, the Encyclical indicates how a "true "ecological debt" (51) exists in the world, with the North in debt to the South. In the face of climate change, there are "differentiated responsibilities" (52), and those of the developed countries are greater.

Aware of the profound differences over these issues, Pope Francis shows himself to be deeply affected by the "weak responses" in the face of the drama of many peoples and populations. Even though there is no lack of positive examples (58), there is "a complacency and a cheerful recklessness" (59). An adequate culture is lacking (53) as well as a willingness to change life style,

4

production and consumption (59), while there are efforts being made "to establish a legal framework which can set clear boundaries and ensure the protection of ecosystems" (53).

Chapter Two – *The Gospel of Creation*

To face the problems illustrated in the previous chapter, Pope Francis selects Biblical accounts, offering a comprehensive view that comes from the Judeo-Christian tradition. With this he articulates the "tremendous responsibility" (90) of humankind for creation, the intimate connection among all creatures and the fact that "the natural environment is a collective good, the patrimony of all humanity and the responsibility of everyone" (95).

In the Bible, "the God who liberates and saves is the same God who created the universe, and these two divine ways of acting are intimately and inseparably connected" (73). The story of creation is central for reflecting on the relationship between human beings and other creatures and how sin breaks the equilibrium of all creation in its entirety: "These accounts suggest that human life is grounded in three fundamental and closely intertwined relationships: with God, with our neighbour and with the earth itself. According to the Bible, these three vital relationships have been broken, both outwardly and within us. This rupture is sin" (66).

For this, even if "we Christians have at times incorrectly interpreted the Scriptures, nowadays we must forcefully reject the notion that our being created in God's image and given dominion over the earth justifies absolute domination over other creatures" (67). Human beings have the responsibility to ""till and keep" the garden of the world (cf. *Gen* 2:15)" (67), knowing that "the ultimate purpose of other creatures is not to be found in us. Rather, all creatures are moving forward, with us and through us, towards a common point of arrival, which is God" (83).

That the human being is not the master of the universe "does not mean to put all living beings on the same level and to deprive human beings of their unique worth and the tremendous responsibility it entails. Nor does it imply a divinization of the earth which would prevent us from working on it and protecting it in its fragility" (90). In this perspective, "every act of cruelty

towards any creature is "contrary to human dignity" (92). However, "a sense of deep communion with the rest of nature cannot be real if our hearts lack tenderness, compassion and concern for our fellow human beings" (91). What is needed is the awareness of a universal communion: "called into being by the one Father. All of us are linked by unseen bonds and together form a kind of universal family, a sublime communion which fills us with a sacred, affectionate and humble respect" (89).

The chapter concludes with the heart of Christian revelation: "The earthly Jesus" with "his tangible and loving relationship with the world" is "risen and glorious, and is present throughout creation by his universal Lordship" (100).

5

Chapter three – *The human roots of the ecological crisis*

This chapter gives an analysis of the current situation, "so as to consider not only its symptoms but also its deepest causes" (15), in a dialogue with philosophy and the human sciences.

Reflections on technology are an initial focus of the chapter: the great contribution to the improvement of living conditions is acknowledged with gratitude. However it gives "those with the knowledge, and especially the economic resources to use them, an impressive dominance over the whole of humanity and the entire world" (104). It is precisely the mentality of technocratic domination that leads to the destruction of nature and the exploitation of people and the most vulnerable populations. "The technocratic paradigm also tends to dominate economics and political life" (109), keeping us from recognizing that "by itself the market cannot guarantee integral human development and social inclusion" (109).

"Modernity has been marked by an excessive anthropocentrism" (116): human beings no long recognize their right place with respect to the world and take on a self-centered position, focused exclusively on themselves and on their own power. This results in a "use and throw away" logic that justifies every type of waste, environmental or human, that treats both the other and nature as simple objects and leads to a myriad of forms of domination. It is this mentality that leads to exploiting children, abandoning the elderly, forcing others into slavery and over-evaluating the capacity of the market to regulate itself, practicing human trafficking, selling pelts of animals in danger of extinction and of "blood diamonds". It is the same mentality as many mafias, of those involved in trafficking organs and drug trafficking and of throwing away unborn babies because they do not correspond to what the parents want (123).

In this light, the Encyclical addresses two crucial problems of today's world. Above all work: "any approach to an integral ecology, which by definition does not exclude human beings, needs to take

account of the value of labour" (124), because "to stop investing in people, in order to gain greater short-term financial gain, is bad business for society" (128).

The second problem regards the limitations of scientific progress, with clear reference to GMOs (132-136). This is a "complex environmental issue" (135). Even though "in some regions their use has brought about economic growth which has helped to resolve problems, there remain a number of significant difficulties which should not be underestimated" (134), starting from the "productive land being concentrated in the hands of a few owners" (134). Pope Francis thinks particularly of small producers and rural workers, of biodiversity, and the network of ecosystems.

Therefore "a broad, responsible scientific and social debate needs to take place, one capable of considering all the available information and of calling things by their name" starting from "lines of independent, interdisciplinary research" (135).

6

Chapter four – *Integral Ecology*

The heart of what the Encyclical proposes is integral ecology as a new paradigm of justice; an ecology "which respects our unique place as human beings in this world and our relationship to our surroundings" (15). In fact, "nature cannot be regarded as something separate from ourselves or as a mere setting in which we live" (139). This is true as we are involved in various fields: in economy and politics, in different cultures particularly in those most threatened, and even in every moment of our daily lives.

The integral perspective also brings the ecology of institutions into play: "if everything is related, then the health of a society's institutions affects the environment and the quality of human life. "Every violation of solidarity and civic friendship harms the environment" (142).

With many concrete examples, Pope Francis confirm his thinking that "the analysis of environmental problems cannot be separated from the analysis of human, family, work-related and urban contexts, and of how individuals relate to themselves" (141). "We are not faced with two separate crises, one environmental and the other social, but rather one complex crisis which is bothsocial and environmental" (139).

"Human ecology is inseparable from the notion of the common good" (156), but is to be understood in a concrete way. In today's context, in which, "injustices abound and growing numbers of people are deprived of basic human rights and considered expendable" (158), committing oneself to the common good means to make choices in solidarity based on a preferential option for the poorest of our brothers and sisters" (158). This is also the best way to leave a sustainable world for future generations, not just by proclaiming, but by committing to care for the poor of today, as already emphasized by Benedict XVI: "In addition to a fairer sense of inter-generational solidarity there is also an urgent moral need for a renewed sense of intragenerational solidarity" (162).

Integral ecology also involves everyday life. The Encyclical gives specific attention to the urban environment. The human being has a great capacity for adaptation and "an admirable creativity and generosity is shown by persons and groups who respond to environmental limitations by alleviating the adverse effects of their surroundings and learning to live productively amid disorder and uncertainty" (148). Nevertheless, authentic development presupposes an integral improvement in the quality of human life: public space, housing, transport, etc. (150-154).

Also "the acceptance of our bodies as God's gift is vital for welcoming and accepting the entire world as a gift from the Father and our common home, whereas thinking that we enjoy

7

absolute power over our own bodies turns, often subtly, into thinking that we enjoy absolute power over creation" (155).

Chapter five – *Lines of approach and action*

This chapter addresses the question of what we can and must do. Analyses are not enough: we need proposals "for dialogue and action which would involve each of us individually no less than international policy" (15). They will "help us to escape the spiral of self-destruction which currently engulfs us" (163). For Pope Francis it is imperative that the developing real approaches is not done in an ideological, superficial or reductionist way. For this, dialogue is essential, a term present in the title of every section of this chapter. "There are certain environmental issues where it is not easy to achieve a broad consensus. [...] the Church does not presume to settle scientific questions or to replace politics. But I want to encourage an honest and open debate, so that particular interests or ideologies will not prejudice the common good" (188).

On this basis, Pope Francis is not afraid to judge international dynamics severely: "Recent World Summits on the environment have failed to live up to expectations because, due to lack of political will, they were unable to reach truly meaningful and effective global agreements on the environment" (166). And he asks "What would induce anyone, at this stage, to hold on to power only to be remembered for their inability to take action when it was urgent and necessary to do so?"

(57). Instead, what is needed, as the Popes have repeated several times, starting with *Pacem in terris*, are forms and instruments for global governance (175): "an agreement on systems of governance for the whole range of the so-called "global commons"" (174), seeing that "environmental protection cannot be assured solely on the basis of financial calculations of costs and benefits. The environment is one of those goods that cannot be adequately safeguarded or promoted by market forces" (190, *Compendium of the Social Doctrine of the Church*).

In this fifth chapter, Pope Francis insists on development of honest and transparent decision making processes, in order to "discern" which policies and business initiatives can bring about

"genuine integral development" (185). In particular, a proper environmental impact study of new

"business ventures and projects demands transparent political processes involving a free exchange of views. On the other hand, the forms of corruption which conceal the actual environmental impact of a given project in exchange for favours usually produce specious agreements which fail to inform adequately and do not allow for full debate" (182).

The most significant appeal is addressed to those who hold political office, so that they avoid

"a mentality of "efficiency" and "immediacy"" (181) that is so prevalent today: "but if they are

8

courageous, they will attest to their God-given dignity and leave behind a testimony of selfless responsibility" (181).

Chapter six – *Ecological education and spirituality*

The final chapter invites everyone to the heart of ecological conversion. The roots of the cultural crisis are deep, and it is not easy to reshape habits and behaviour. Education and training are the key challenges: "change is impossible without motivation and a process of education" (15).

All educational sectors are involved, primarily "at school, in families, in the media, in catechesis and elsewhere" (213).

The starting point is "to aim for a new lifestyle" (203-208), which also opens the possibility of "bringing healthy pressure to bear on those who wield political, economic and social power" (206).

This is what happens when consumer choices are able to "change the way businesses operate, forcing them to consider their environmental footprint and their patterns of production" (206).

The importance of environmental education cannot be underestimated. It is able to affect actions and daily habits, the reduction of water consumption, the sorting of waste up and even

"turning off unnecessary lights" (211): "An integral ecology is also made up of simple daily gestures which break with the logic of violence, exploitation and selfishness" (230). Everything will be easier starting with a contemplative outlook that comes from faith: "as believers, we do not look at the world from without but from within, conscious of the bonds with which the Father has linked us with all beings. By developing our individual, God-given capacities, an ecological conversion can inspire us to greater creativity and enthusiasm" (220).

As proposed in *Evangelii Gaudium:* "sobriety, when lived freely and consciously, is liberating" (223), just as "happiness means knowing how to limit some needs which only diminish us, and being open to the many different possibilities which life can offer" (223). In this way "we must regain the conviction that we need one another, that we have a shared responsibility for others and the world, and that being good and decent are worth it" (229).

The saints accompany us on this journey. Saint Francis, cited several times, is "the example par excellence of care for the vulnerable and of an integral ecology lived out joyfully and authentically" (10). He is the model of "the inseparable bond between concern for nature, justice for the poor, commitment to society, and interior peace" (10). The Encyclical also mentions Saint Benedict, Saint Teresa di Lisieux and Blessed Charles de Foucauld.

After *Laudato si'*, the regular practice of an examination of conscience, the means that the Church has always recommended to orient one's life in light of the relationship with the Lord,

9

should include a new dimension, considering not only how one has lived communion with God,

with others and with oneself, but also with all creatures and with nature.

A prayer for our earth

A Christian prayer in union with creation

Appendix2: To the Roots of the "spirit of Assisi" [197]

I understand that no one could ignore October 27, 1986.

That day I brought about curiosity, questions, and expectations . . . This is the reason why many ask:

Who are you? What do you want? Good question!

John Paul II knew me very well and he described me in this way: "that men and women perceptive to religious values assist others to find joy and determination to walk together"

Instead, I prefer the following words that are more explicit:

Moved by the example of St. Francis and St. Clare, true disciples of Christ, and convinced by the experience of this day that we have lived together, we (representatives of different religious dominations and religious communities reunited at Assisi),

commit ourselves to examine our consciences, to faithfully listen to this voice and purify our spirit from prejudice, hatred, hostility, jealousy and envy. We will search to be peace makers in thought and action, with our minds and hearts attentive to the humanity of the human family.

We invite all of our brothers and sisters that listen to us to do the same.

We do so mindful of our human limits and aware that we will fail. We must recognize, therefore, that our future peace always depends on a gift that God grants us.

In this spirit, we invite world leaders to take our humble supplication to God for peace.

We likewise request that they recognize their responsibility and dedicate themselves with renewed commitment to peace, courageously and wisely putting into action peace keeping plans.

These words of the Holy Father describe my identity very beautifully.

He spoke of me in many different occasions and after him followed many others, such as those of the Church, journalists, and especially Franciscans.

Thereafter, I received the universal name spirit of Assisi.

In other words, I would say that I am a commitment asked by all people to purify their spirit from prejudices, hatred, hostility, jealousy, and envy.

---

[197] From the CEFID :

I implore all humankind to live fraternally and in solidarity; to be peace builders in thought and in deed, in mind and in heart, mindful of their human limits and acknowledging that peace is always a gift of od.

On that day in 1986, all of these values were proposed through the concrete means of prayer, fasting, pilgrimage and silence.

When my identity was interpreted by others, it received various accentuations:

-for some I signify following that which unites without noting the risks or having fear to encounter diversity, being mindful of the common desire, origin and happiness that we are all called to;
- for others I call to mind an ecumenical disposition that invites "all persons, whatever race or language, from all nations and every part of the earth", to recognize that "everything comes from the Most High Lord God ", especially the passionate search for peace among religions of the world;
- still for others I represent the continual prayer to obtain the gift of peace from God; the contemplation that allows one to discern the presence and creative action of the Word of God and of his Spirit in every initiative regarding peace, reconciliation and fraternity;
- for others the "spirit of Assisi" had and continues to have a fundamental role in ecumenism;
- still for others I have the mission to "reunite all religions and

Message of John Paul II to Cardinal Edward Cassidy in occasion of the encounter organized at Assisi by the Community7 September 1994.

Appendix 3: A Prayer for our Earth, and a (Christian) Prayer in Union with Creation

A Prayer for our Earth

By Pope Francis*

All-powerful God, you are present in the whole universe
and in the smallest of your creatures.
You embrace with your tenderness all that exists.
Pour out upon us the power of your love,
that we may protect life and beauty.
Fill us with peace, that we may live
as brothers and sisters, harming no one.
O God of the poor,
help us to rescue the abandoned and forgotten of this earth,
so precious in your eyes.
Bring healing to our lives,
that we may protect the world and not prey on it,
that we may sow beauty, not pollution and destruction.
Touch the hearts
of those who look only for gain
at the expense of the poor and the earth.
Teach us to discover the worth of each thing,
to be filled with awe and contemplation,
to recognize that we are profoundly united
with every creature
as we journey towards your infinite light.
We thank you for being with us each day.
Encourage us, we pray, in our struggle
for justice, love and peace .
* Pope Francis published this prayer in his Laudato Si' encyclical, and is meant for sharing with all who believe in a God who is the all-powerful Creator .

A Christian prayer in union with creation

By Pope Francis*

Father, we praise you with all your creatures.
They came forth from your all-powerful hand;
they are yours, filled with your presence and your tender love.
Praise be to you!
Son of God, Jesus,
through you all things were made.
You were formed in the womb of Mary our Mother,
you became part of this earth,
and you gazed upon this world with human eyes.
Today you are alive in every creature
in your risen glory.
Praise be to you!
Holy Spirit, by your light
you guide this world towards the Father's love
and accompany creation as it groans in travail.
You also dwell in our hearts
and you inspire us to do what is good.
Praise be to you!
Triune Lord, wondrous community of infinite love,
teach us to contemplate you
in the beauty of the universe,
for all things speak of you.
Awaken our praise and thankfulness
for every being that you have made.
Give us the grace to feel profoundly joined
to everything that is.
God of love, show us our place in this world
as channels of your love
for all the creatures of this earth,
for not one of them is forgotten in your sight.
Enlighten those who possess power and money
that they may avoid the sin of indifference,
that they may love the common good, advance the weak,
and care for this world in which we live.
The poor and the earth are crying out.
O Lord, seize us with your power and light,
help us to protect all life,
to prepare for a better future,
for the coming of your Kingdom
of justice, peace, love and beauty.
Praise be to you!
Amen.
* Pope Francis published this prayer in his Laudato Si' encyclical, and is meant for us Christians to ask for inspiration to take up the commitment to creation set before us by the Gospel of Jesus.

Recommended Background Material

TOP Video Presentations, Websites, Reports and Websites

1. www.EnergyandStuff.org
2. The Age of Sustainable Development
3. The Great Acceleration- video
4. The Great Acceleration- website and scientific articles
5. The Sustainable Development Goals- official website, knowledge platform
6. The Sustainable Development Goals- powerslides
7. Pope Francis Encyclical- Laudato Si!- Care for Creation and our Common Home
8. Davos WEF 2017: An Insight. An Idea –with Cardinal Pietro Parolin
9. Davos WEF2017: The Crisis of the Middle-Class
10. Better Business- Better World

Some sample documents from Energy For One World

Presentation to Executive Energy Leaders - by Energy For One World (powerslides only)

Webcast presentation on the Year 2015-2016 Agenda

The Global Change Challenge

Energy Architecture, Integral Ecology, Society, Economy and our Transition Management

Walking on the Path of Sustainable Development

Leadership, Leadership of Change

Tales of Conversion

Articles shared at Global Conferences on UN SDSN:

- Energy & Sustainable Development- The Realization of a new global compact on Energy Architecture Development
- New Roles and Responsibilities for Business in the UN Sustainable Development Goals
-

www.energyforoneworld.com

Weekly Insights

www.energyforoneworld.com